Frankston Library Service

Please return items by the date printed on your loans docket.
To renew a loan, quote date items are due
and your card number.
Fees are charged for items returned late.

60 PLAYNE STREET FRANKSTON VICTORIA AUSTRALIA 3199
TELEPHONE 03 9784 1020 FAX 03 9783 2616
CARRUM DOWNS LIBRARY 203 LYREBIRD DRIVE
TELEPHONE 03 9782 0418

Catherine

Catherine

On Catherine Currie's Diary, 1873–1908

Ailsa McLeary

with Tony Dingle

MELBOURNE UNIVERSITY PRESS

Melbourne University Press
PO Box 278, Carlton South, Victoria 3053, Australia
info@mup.unimelb.edu.au
www.mup.com.au

First published 1998

Designed by Melissa Graham
Typeset in Malaysia
by Syarikat Seng Teik Sdn. Bhd.
in 11/14 point Elegant Garamond
Printed in Australia by RossCo Print.

National Library of Australia Cataloguing-in-Publication entry
McLeary, Ailsa.
   Catherine: on Catherine Currie's diary, 1873–1908
   Bibliography.
   Includes index.
   ISBN 0 522 84836 2.

   1. Currie, Catherine—Diaries. 2. Currie family. 3. Women
   pioneers—Victoria—Gippsland—Diaries. 4. Buln Buln
   (Vic.: Shire)—History. I. Currie, Catherine. II. Dingle, A. E.
   (Anthony Edward), 1942– . III. Title.
994.56

Frontispiece: Catherine, John and baby Albert Bryce Currie, photographed by Lind photographers, Bourke
Street, when the family visited Melbourne in 1875 on their way to take up their selection at Lardner.

Contents

Illustrations

A Note on the Diary

Catherine's diary was found by the architect and historian Graeme Butler when he was researching his history of the Buln Buln shire. When Catherine's daughter Fern Currie died in 1968 she left some of the family land to the Warragul Field Days organisation; one of the directors saved the seven large foolscap books, containing the account of Catherine's life, found on the property. Butler used excerpts from the diary in his history of Buln Buln, and then ensured that it was sent to Catherine's grandson, and a copy placed in the State Library of Victoria. The diary has been mined for information on pioneering life, farm labour and the Gippsland community.

Although permission must be sought to use the diary, it has now become public knowledge, and historical artefact. It is carefully preserved; it is precious because it is old and unique. Even before it was old it was valuable, and it must have been precious to the Currie family in order to survive all the vicissitudes of their hard pioneering life. The diary was begun when the family was at Ballan, and it was packed with the most essential family possessions that made the long trip to Lardner. The books may have presented a problem of space in the first tiny wooden hut crowded with two adults and three small children, and even in a later, larger house built for a family of seven. The family moved house several times, and all the volumes travelled with them. One of the houses they had temporarily vacated was burned to the ground in a bushfire, but the diary was safely stored at the current abode.

Catherine's few spelling mistakes have not been corrected during transcription. Some small amendments have been made to render the meaning clearer to the reader; for example, upper-case letters inserted where Catherine used lower case at the beginning of sentences. Words underlined by Catherine are indicated by a change of font.

Acknowledgements

John Currie, who possesses the original diary of Catherine Currie, kindly allowed us to use it and encouraged us in our research. Charles Fahey read the diary and indicated its breadth and importance to us. Betty and Bruce Hedley reminisced about Lardner and the Curries, and identified the site of the first house. Robert and Bev Berry kindly allowed us to look around the second house and the outbuildings, which they now own and are preserving. Bill McFerran supplied photographs and much useful information. Colin Silcock unearthed valuable references, and the only photograph we have of Catherine. Sally Wilde shared her discoveries about Warragul and district, and Meredith Fletcher enthused about everything pertaining to Gippsland and its history. We are indebted to the Australian Research Grants Council for a small grant in 1988, and to the Faculty of Art, Design and Communication at the Royal Melbourne Institute of Technology and to Monash University for assistance with publishing costs. Sally Esse of the *Works* Graphic Design consultancy at RMIT provided the original design for the selection map and family tree. Lastly we wish to acknowledge the patience of the many people who have listened to us telling Catherine's story.

Conversions

1 foot	0.30 metre
1 pound (lb)	0.45 kilogram
1 hundredweight	50.80 kilograms
1 ton	1.02 tonnes
1 acre	0.40 hectare
1 gallon	4.55 litres
1 bushel (8 gallons)	36.4 litres
1 pound (£)	20 shillings (s)
1 crown	5s
1s	12 pence (d)
£1	$2 (1968 conversion)

Prelude

The island continent is vibrant red at the centre, fading outwards through ochre and yellow to gold, grass green, aquamarine and the sapphire blue where sharks circle. In the natural landscape there are points where one colour begins to fade almost imperceptibly into another. Despite their beauty, such places on the continent are sparsely populated, for people seem generally uneasy with ambiguities and prefer to live within the definite category. They do not often pitch a tent or build a city on a place which looks like a boundary between two choices. People set up in designated cattle or sheep country, or establish themselves in places delineated by a symbolic title such as 'the outback' or 'the goldfields'. The names and categories define occupation and habit as well as landscape and habitat, and lives are ordered by the function of a place as well as its colour and form.

The original human inhabitants once had different boundaries, and a land circumscribed by different names and functions. The people moved only hesitantly outside their own and well-known territory, aware of the dangers of trespassing on another's land. When the first Europeans arrived they considered this pristine land a *terra nullius*, for it seemed to be empty of language and edifice, symbol and structure. Later they would learn that over two hundred and fifty different languages were spoken on the continent before the English tongue invaded, and that both concepts and objects were not only already named, but were surrounded by complex stories and implications.

But at the beginning of white settlement, it would be the words and concepts of dominant strangers that would establish the new map of the landscape. The people who arrived from the wet green islands of the northern hemisphere had evolved in a different climate and among different colours. Huddled on the coastal edge, the new Australians only gradually came to terms with the breadth and depth of their land, and the fact that all unknown landscapes, even those that are the colour of life, are dangerous.

The first explorers and colonisers attempted to render the new land safer and more familiar by bestowing well-known names. The green and blue south-east corner of the continent was named by the explorer Angus McMillan as Caledonia Australia, because it reminded him of his native Scotland. On 27 March 1840 Count Strzelecki arrived at Numbla-Mungee, and suggested to McMillan that the new country should be named Gippsland in honour of the New South Wales Governor.[1] So easily were two levels of ancient poetry reduced to prose. Yet the prosaic name enclosed an area of the continent that would become the subject of more than its share of poetry and metaphor.

At the beginning, the name surrounded an absence: an absence of knowledge, an absence of myth, an absence of history. Most of all, however, it was an absence of words. The pioneers of Gippsland saw their aim as civilising the land by cutting down the forest and turning it into a familiar and domesticated landscape. In the manner of the time, it would be a man-made landscape, with woman-made trimmings. Once explorers had given the name of Gippsland, it was necessary for settlers to invent a place to fit the name, to change the *terra incognita* to a place called home.

Even before the Great Southern Land had been found, it had been necessary to invent it. It already existed on maps as some sort of inchoate shape which would balance the bulk of the northern hemisphere. This absent continent was the necessary Antipodes, the antithesis and antidote to Europe. But once found, *terra australis* became more than a metaphor, and more complicated than a virtual reality. The land now had a shape and a colour, a name and a form. It would have to be mapped as multi-hued and varied; it had a third dimension, for it spread not only horizontally from sea to sea, but rose vertically in the form of forests and mountain ranges. This was now the real thing, a living land with a proper name.

For migrants from the old country, the world had turned. Europe was now the 'necessary antipodes, underwriting all our myths of absence'.[2] In Europe, the idea of absence consisted of the destruction of an existing presence; the idea of conquest was predicated in part on destroying a visible culture in order to demoralise the conquered. This destruction created a palpable 'absence' which could then be filled with another, superior or dominant presence. After one of the greatest periods of destruction in its modern history, Europe surveyed part of the 'No Man's Land' it had created. Considering the Potsdamer Platz in the centre of Berlin, formerly a part of the most vibrant city centre in Europe and now converted by war to a 'vast field of rubble', Richard Weller says,

> The irony and peculiar beauty of No Man's Land is its linguistic density and its actual emptiness. No Man's Land holds the potential of that which is not yet written. It is the missing paragraph—an absence into which ever more dubious rhetoric is projected.[3]

Australia however, the antithesis of Europe, was actual density and linguistic emptiness. There was an unease about this perceived 'absence', this lack of something which had been consciously and culturally formed, and which could be consciously and systematically destroyed in order to fill it with another presence. Here there were no lingering symbols to play with, no density which would give meaning to absence, and therefore no possibility even for irony. Perhaps the new Australians were half aware that there was a dream hanging over the land that had not been properly destroyed, and which might reappear at another time, demanding to be reconciled. This, however, was not a concept easily put into words.

For the moment, the linguistic emptiness would have to be filled with old and transplanted words. The confident words of the first English speakers filled the land with new names, the words and meanings of those who did not yet understand the boundaries, the form or the power of a continent which already had its own cosmogony. Philip Mead has said that 'our cosmogony expresses itself in vocabularies of heraldry and geography and in taxonomies of time'.[4] The integrity of those who first settled the land depended on classifying and naming plants and the animals, on measuring rainfall and the height of mountains, on finding the age of the continent, on creating the density that only language could bestow. This would give a new harmony and wholeness to a landscape that had developed its colour and form by a slow and wordless process of natural selection over millions of years.

This ordering and naming was a human process, based on the cacophony of many voices. To take one voice may give a singular picture of the conversation that was part of the march of progress and the evolution of a new landscape. One singular narrative exists in the diary of one of the pioneers of Gippsland, Catherine Currie. She had moved from England to the goldfields of Australia at the age of seven, on an involuntary journey prescribed by her parents. From the goldfields she moved with her family to the small town of Bacchus Marsh, and travelled on to the surrounding plains of Ballan with her Scottish husband, whose values and vocabulary she adopted with ease. With him and her own small family she moved on to Lardner, and the great green forest that rose vertically around her, dwarfing her with its silence and power.

Her journeys, both voluntary and involuntary, kept taking her further and further away from the centre of the world she knew. Her husband had a clear function—he and his sons would clear the forest to create a farm. Catherine's function was less clear. She would raise a family, but she would also converse with the new country in order to fill this unknown absence with her presence. This is exactly what she did.

There is now a chorus of voices, filling the silent land with comment on commentary, with ideas and concepts and specific narratives. Catherine's diary is one small commentary without irony, for it began almost as a list of experiences, an immediate and direct account of a life. It encloses the experience of one woman, one voice at the centre of the world. It was a monologue, now turned to dialogue as we project our own, perhaps dubious, rhetoric. Now we know that every landscape is dangerous, perhaps especially one which you have created for yourself and enclosed with words.

Context

In the nineteenth century, before everything turned into the con-
venience of bland, blanched paper or plastic, the colour of money was
gold. The colours of the island continent stretched from one horizon
to another, but the colours also ran in deep and vertical layers. Beneath
the surface rested several treasures, and the first of these was the
shiniest, the heaviest and best to hold in the human hand. White
Australia had begun as a prison for exiles and misfits, outcasts and
mavericks. Out at the boundary of civilisation, its newly discovered
treasures soon made it the Mecca for colourful adventurers, that other
brand of people set on smashing the old boundaries that separated the
rulers from the ruled, the rich from the poor.

Respectable people arrived later and more cautiously, wishing to be
rich without crossing too many of the boundaries that their cultural
training had imposed. These boundaries they carried within them like
a weight and around them like an aura. Their integrity consisted of
wholeness, soundness, uprightness and honesty taught by a culture
that imagined that these things were necessary to the completeness of
a whole. One of these cautious adventurers was John Currie, who had
been born near Edinburgh in 1834. In 1854 he packed his strong
Scottish values along with the small amount of other baggage he

carried on to the famous clipper ship, *Champion of the Seas*, for the voyage to Australia. To Melbourne and then on to the Ballarat diggings he carried his immortal but prosaic Presbyterian soul and his desire for riches. He saw no contradiction or ambiguity in his quest for both spiritual and worldly wealth.

He did not find enough gold to make him a rich man, but he did unearth a wife to endow with all his worldly goods and a great many of his values. Sarah Ann Catherine Wells had been born in Ipswich, England, in 1845, and was only seven years old when she sailed with her family on the *Calphurnia*, reaching the goldfields in 1853. Catherine had a father named Leaper Hurry Wells, a name which may have forced upon him a more prodigal and impulsive nature than that possessed by the solid John Currie. Catherine was one of a family of twelve children, and when the fertile breadwinner of the family found no gold, the ten progeny who survived the rigours of birth and childhood in the new colony were supported on Leaper's wage as a brickmaker. In 1864 Leaper's wife Elizabeth died after the birth of her twelfth child.*

Catherine, the second daughter of Leaper and Elizabeth, married John Currie in a Ballarat church in the year of her mother's early death. It may be that at the age of nineteen she married not only to escape the impending and imposing child-minding duties but also to exchange a disordered life for one of more structure and purpose. Her husband, eleven years older than she, ambitious, Scottish and upright, might have been expected to provide more worldly and spiritual goods

---

* The children were Leaper, who died in infancy, Elizabeth, Catherine, George, Alice, Leaper, Caroline, Jane, Edward, Annie and John. On 27 January 1864 the mother Elizabeth died of puerperal fever after the birth of a daughter, Keziah Rebecca. The baby girl died fifteen days later. The eldest daugher Lizzie, aged twenty, was now in charge of nine younger brothers and sisters, the youngest aged only two.

than she could expect at home. The fact that the Currie's first child, Elizabeth, was born eight months after the marriage could charitably be put down to a premature birth.

John Currie had travelled from the United Kingdom in search of gold and a new life. It is probable that he did find some gold, and enough hope to keep searching for the elusive metal even when he had become an established farmer. As a true Lowland Scot, he had turned his efforts to the next precious resource offered by the colony. By the end of 1856 John's elder brother James had joined him in the colony, and between this year and 1863 John had made the transition from miner to farmer. By 1863 he was renting 120 acres of land near Ballan, and he then selected 90 acres of land at Parwan, near Bacchus Marsh. This selection was an unwise choice as the land turned out to be poor, and John transferred it to a neighbouring farmer, charging him only expenses.

In December 1865 John Currie selected another 114 acres at Ballan in the parish of Gorong. It was to this selection, which they named 'Woodmuir', that Catherine and John moved with their first child. Elizabeth Bryce Currie had been born in May 1865, but tragedy struck when she died of inflammation of the throat just after her first birthday. In April 1867 Catherine (Katie) was born, followed in August 1869 by Thomas Bryce (Tom).

In 1873 the Curries moved on to the forest of Gippsland, to take up a new selection at Lardner, on the south-east edge of the continent. In reflection of a past life, they would name their Gippsland house 'Brandie Braes', a name from John's boyhood home in West Calder. The greenness of the forest, the first settlers thought, indicated good soil and fertility, as it had in the old country. They were perhaps only partly aware that this Australian forest would require extraordinary efforts before it could be transformed into a landscape resembling the quiet pastures of Britain.

Hard work and effort were no deterrent to the Currie family and other settlers in the forest. Looking back on the lives of his pioneer ancestors, Gippsland-born historian Don Watson says of them,

> The selectors cut farms out of blue gum and mountain ash forests in a labour that now looks superhuman. The children worked as hard as the adults. They did this not simply to make a living—that was something which could have been done much more easily in the cities. They did it to achieve what they imagined would be dignity and respectability. Some of them would have called it grace.[5]

The Curries, like the other selectors, were aware of their role as pioneers, and conscious of its implications. They were among the last of the new settlers in a land that had already made the pioneer a mythical figure, an ordinary person who nevertheless completed the task of bringing civilisation to a savage environment and creating order out of chaos. What the pioneers sought was the creation of normal life, as they had always understood it. Watson says,

> the idea of Gippsland is the idea of the normal. That is what pioneering is—the quest for normality, a set of unwritten rules by which a community lives. This is a radical enterprise, particularly when you realize what that normality encompasses.[6]

Catherine Currie, Australian pioneer, kept a meticulous diary of her life from 1873 until her death in 1908. Working from her list of unwritten rules, she set out to fill the linguistic emptiness with the normality of her words, and to write the Currie story as a narrative of progress. This was a record of an enterprise she accepted without question as being valuable and important. Her chronological narrative would make sense of a world and a life that was wild and sometimes out of her control. Her story would restore an order and a form, give a veneer of normality, a clothing of literate virtue that might almost be called grace.

Catherine was living on the edge of the written and the unwritten, and sometimes on the boundary between imagination and reality. Her narrative was designed to be a serene and chronological sequence, complete with the happy ending that such an enterprise deserved. But she could not have foreseen the discontinuities of her narrative, which would carry her to a destination she had not expected. As the years wore on, the diary Catherine was keeping changed in a subtle way. From the calm and assured story of a pioneering family battling the natural wilderness in order to impose their own normality, it became more and more a refuge for the thoughts of an isolated woman struggling to make sense of herself as well as the strange world she had come to inhabit. Catherine now sometimes confided that she would need to hide her diary, for it was becoming too personal to leave out on a table for the perusal of her family and other strangers. It was becoming the story of an inner as well as an outer life, of a battle Catherine was waging between grace and disgrace.

In the first years of diary-keeping, the current book lay open on a table, accessible to any member of the family. It was a record of days of planting and reaping, amounts received for butter sold, bills paid for seed and stock, farm implements lent to or borrowed from neighbours. The books were well used, and the volumes now bear marks of the passage of time. Leather spines are partly detached or missing, pages are loose, some stitched, others held together with metal staples that have rusted and discoloured the paper. The writing, originally in black ink, has faded to watery brown, the once-bright purple letters are now a dusty lavender. Yet the writing is bold and the vocabulary simple and clear. Only the hard or unusual word is misspelled; for example, both Catherine and John use *hypocrisy* with some intensity, but both have

Dec 5th I am still at Grants as they cant get any
one else – I do not like this at all Grants
comenced to cut the rye grass has very hot
John rolling and planting turnips – and friend
planting the potatoes   brought the ...
6 John harrowing and doing odd jobs at Grants
7 Mr and Mrs Johnstone came to day Carrie
with them – I have not been home since wednesday
night till 9 oclock to day – John pulled a lot
of strawberries for jam made it in the evening
himself – Mr Lynch up this evening about a
letter from the surveyor about some land
8 very hot John cut the rye grass and
James found it I came home to night
at 12 oclock = had a plate full of strawberries
and cream after I had been in bed very tired
9 John went to Ballan to get Damsel
shod = for a trip to Melbourne = Mr Lynch
shewing the sheep in the evening very
hard work John got an awful warning
10 John started for Melbourne at 2 oclock
a Mr Lynch with him very hot Brennan
set fire to the grass on the hill Jane helping
me wash at Grants = Miss Williamson
here to put off our visit to Mr hossops
11 John came home to day or night 12 oclock
brought tea and sugar sago and raisins £10. worth
for the reaping machine paid for the Crown
Grant for our land did not get it have with him

A typical page, a standard day: Catherine's diary, 5 December 1874 trouble spelling it. This is an exception, for the Curries were proudly literate people.*

Occasionally, scribbled pencil notes on scraps of paper are inter-leaved in the diary, indicating that sometimes entries were stored up and the reports for several days filled in at one sitting. The Curries were not people who had large amounts of leisure time that could be spent composing witty notes for their diary. To read the words now carefully preserved in the silent calm of the State Library is to enter a world of physical work and activity that is almost incomprehensible to the modern reader. It is to conjure up an image of a weary woman sitting under the pale inverted cone of light from a kerosene lamp, a lamp that she herself has carefully filled, which she herself must clean in the morning. The woman who sits writing has finished her work for the day, and her warm bed is waiting to receive her for the few short hours before the dawn milking.

This is a diary that cost something to write. It was begun with hope, and in the faith that the pioneering life, and a written account of it, was useful and important. It is also a diary which costs something to read, for it is not always interesting to the modern reader, filled as it is with the record of hard and repetitive toil. Initially there were no doubts in Catherine's mind that she was inventing her new and strange life by recording it. Biographer Janet Malcolm has said that 'we all invent ourselves, but some of us are more persuaded than others by the fiction that we are interesting'.[7] In Catherine's case, she was sure that her world was interesting. She recorded everything: sales and prices, work and rainfall, the visits of family and neighbours. Sitting precariously at the edge of the continent, her words surrounded her

---

* Catherine had spent many days at school, even though her school days were over before legislation introduced compulsory education to Victoria.

family with comfort and normality. Until life refused to be normal, and she, small and lonely in her giant forest, found that words could become disconnected from their meanings at the frontier of the written and the unwritten, and that ambiguities would always emerge from between the lines.

Catherine Currie was engaged in a radical enterprise, placed somewhere on the boundary of an ambiguity that could not be expressed because not yet recognised. Hidden deep in the forest at the edge of the world, the Curries and their neighbours would spend their lives hacking at the ferns and vines and enormous trees that had formed over thousands of years, to change it to the pale green and gold of well-fenced pastures and fields of grain. Their puny but single-minded efforts would change the course of evolution, for there were enough members of this dominant human species to destroy an ancient harmony. The survival of the fittest was no longer the product of natural serendipity, but the result of choices made by the deliberate human actor at the centre of the world.

Catherine Currie lived at the furthest boundary of the civilised world, and yet she was at the centre of her own world. At the edge of the written and the unwritten, she created a narrative of which she was the mid-point and the central character. Elias Canetti says,

> I know people who make fun of other people's calendars, because 'there's so little in them'. But only the man who has made one for himself can truly know what's in it. The leanness of these signs makes up their value. They exist by dint of their concentration, they are well-nigh magically sealed, they are unused and can suddenly grow into something enormous through other proximities in some other year.
>
> Now there is no living person who would not have the right to such memo books. *Everyone* is the midpoint of the world, absolutely everyone, and the world is precious only because it is full of such midpoints. That is the *meaning* of the

word 'human': each person a midpoint next to countless others, who are mid-points as much as he.[8]

Or as much as she. This is a woman's account, mediated through the context of her time which dictated that the masculine world of work and public service was more important than the woman's domestic role. Yet it is the voice of Catherine that tells this story, with husband John a shadowy but commanding figure in the background.

Catherine Currie was the midpoint of her own narrative, as she is the midpoint of this one. There was a human cost in filling the linguistic absence with the presence of her words, in mapping the boundaries between the written and the unwritten, in being a woman in No Man's Land, in establishing the idea of the normal. It was people like Catherine Currie who paid this cost. As she and John cut and burned their way through the great forest towards the pale pastures that represented wealth and serenity, she was often circled by ribbons of fire. As she fenced her family in with boundaries that would keep them safe from snakes and 'bears' and other people, she was not too far from the edge of the continent that was furthest from home. Out beyond the boundaries imposed by her words, the beautiful ambiguities remained: the green merged into aquamarine, and the aquamarine changed to the sapphire blue where sharks circled.

Journeys 1873–1875

1873

On 8 March 1873 Ballan selector John Currie drove into Ballarat in a borrowed spring cart to do some buying and selling. One of his purchases was an empty, lined journal. When he arrived home, he recorded his day's work:

> *At Ballarat in Landers spring cart and bought 4 pigs at 1£ each, bought this book. Some 2 copies Book and second sequel for Katie all for 9/6. Got a new hat took some bacon and sold it for 9/– per lb spiced. Got home about 12 o'clock PM.*

It is a suitably prosaic and representative first entry from this laconic farmer who had always had more time for deeds than for words. In the month of March John recorded that he was ploughing and threshing rye-grass, making a pigsty and fencing, and cutting Indian corn for hay. His wife, whom he nearly always called Kate in the diary, was milking and making butter, winning a first prize for her duck eggs at the show, looking after five-year-old Katie and four-year-old Tom, and making a coat and waistcoat for John. She also did many errands, returning the spring cart to the Landers on 10 March, and taking a load of wheat to the mill five days later. Unfortunately, 'the miller told her there was too many oats in it to make flour'.

Catherine's father still lived at nearby Bacchus Marsh, and her seventeen-year-old sister Jane spent most of her time staying with the Curries at Woodmuir. John's brother James worked on a farm at nearby Ingliston, and he also lived with John's family, helping Catherine with the lighter work. There was a school for the children and church on Sunday. Both Catherine and John enjoyed regular visits to Ballan to attend sales and collect their mail and newspapers. The large market town of Ballarat was also near by.

Neighbours were constantly calling or being visited, and there was much borrowing and lending of farm equipment and spring carts, bartering and selling of produce, and exchange of labour. On 11 March Jane went to stay at Johnston's farm while Mrs Johnston was away, and a week later Catherine went over to help make up the butter. Jane came home again on 23 March. John frequently mentioned visits to and from the Lander, Johnston, Lynch, Wilkinson and Grant families. Such close relationships were not always without friction, especially for a farmer as blunt and parsimonious as John Currie. In March he had an altercation with Alexander (Sandy) and Lachlan Grant.

20.3 *Mr. Grant brought his account but he overcharges me in everything.*

21.3 *L. Grant at me nothing new.*

22.3 *A. Grant came over. I told him that his Account was wrong that he had charged me for everything too much that the mare was just double what we agreed for £1 10s. He charged me £3 and says that he will swear to it. I just gave him an idea what I thought of him this few years. I wonder what he thinks of it.*

Sandy Grant obviously didn't dwell on the rebuke, for harmonious relations were soon re-established: 'Grant sent me a letter rather a curiosity in its way, being apologetic and rather severe. They are busy valuing their stock and implements'. [24.3]

The Grants were frequent visitors, especially Sandy, who often came over to the Currie farm to have a drink and a chat and, according to Catherine, to 'hinder the work'. In 1873 the Grants were preparing to take up a new selection at Brandy Creek in west Gippsland. In April, John recorded that Lachlan Grant had selected 320 acres, and on 24 April he noted that all accounts between the Curries and the Grants had been settled.

24.4   *A. Grant. Settled up accounts with him quite satisfactorily. Gave him 8 pounds, the mare is scratched out. I do not know if I will have to pay yet but he says no.*

Two days later it was sale day at Ballan, and John took 'Kate and the cart'. He carried out several transactions on his visit to Ballan.

Took 2 Bags of Grass for Mr Johnston and one for J. Conroy, paid for oats and got money for Dan. After squaring I got 17 pounds leaving the rye grass to pay for. Kate bought a pair of trousers and cap for Tom some rum and spirits got James Boots 18s. Cattle there was very few. Coulter refused £8 for a cow, not a great sale—box of pencils bottle of ink.

At the end of April some welcome rain arrived, and the children stayed home from school. John, who had had a bad cold, noted that 'I am a great deal better looking at the water'. Like many farmers, John often recovered from minor ailments as soon as the weather improved.

On 1 May John recorded, 'Jane washing, James in the hole'. James was often listed as being in the hole; he and John had a mining licence, and it seems that they dug shafts on their own property and sometimes elsewhere. On 2 May John wrote to the Mining Board and the Minister of Agriculture, killed two pigs and went to Ballan to see Blake about the roads. John was interested and involved in local affairs, especially when they concerned his own interests. The shire had plans to build a road through his property, and John was doing his best to avert the inevitable: on 19 May he went to Ballan 'to hear the Council about the road—the Engineer reported but the Councillors did nothing'. John was now ploughing land for potatoes, sowing oats and digging artichokes. He was also petitioning for a new school and attending Council meetings.

All these daily activities look like the actions of a man committed to the future of his own farm and locality. John seemed to be prosperously settled at Ballan, and he had paid for his selection in full by 1873. The family was making a good living, and what had been one of the frontiers of selection had now settled into the steady seasonal routines of earning a living from the soil. But beyond the circle of daily activities extended some larger ripples. John was not content with one property, and he had been renting 120 acres of land since at least 1863. The family was building a new dairy and extending the house, and on 13 May the surveyor had come and 'marked out our Residence'. It appears that as well as extending the old house they were ready to build another.

It is not clear from the diary what all this frenetic expansionist activity portended. Perhaps a staid and settled life was too boring for people who had taken the large gamble of leaving home for a new life. Neighbours were already preparing to leave for the next frontier, and on 2 June, John 'saw Mr Selby and arranged to go to Gippsland to look for land, saw A.L. Grant and Bookless'. The next day he 'went to see

Mr Grant about the road to Brandy Creek', and on 4 June he set off for Gippsland on a borrowed horse, but did not get far as Selby's horse 'knocked up'. He had to 'turn in at the Marsh' and settle for a second-hand account of the land from Wilkinson, a neighbour who had been to the area. He went home to dig some artichokes, and on 6 June 'got a letter from E Steadman telling me that Janet Black was dead'. Janet Black was John's stepmother, and now letters began to flow back and forth between Scotland and Ballan. On 10 June John's brother-in-law David Simpson wrote from Adelaide, no doubt seeking information about the death.*

On 13 June John noted that there was an election for the Board of Advice for Education, and he went to Ballan to vote and get the papers. On 18 June he 'Went to Gordon—Land board . . . my case did not come on'. He spent the rest of the month fencing and planting. The whole family was heavily engaged in local affairs, and it seems that John did much of the official correspondence for the community. Katie and Tom were at school, but stayed at home when the weather was bad, as it was too far to travel. Local families were trying to organise a site for a school to serve the immediate neighbourhood, and on 29 June the diary noted that 'Mr Lander here with a promise from Mr Inglis for land for school'. The next day John wrote to the

---

* James and Jean also came to Australia, but apparently not at the same time as John. James was twelve years older than John and arrived in Victoria in 1856. He married Ellen Phillips in 1858, when he was thirty-six and she was forty-three. There were no children of this late marriage, and Ellen died on 6 June 1870 at the age of fifty-five. She is not mentioned in the diary, although Catherine occasionally records James's visits to the cemetery. Jean Currie married David Simpson, who had also travelled to Australia aboard *Champion of the Seas*, and the Simpsons lived in Adelaide. The Currie parents apparently did not come to Australia. After the death of his first wife Elizabeth, Thomas married Janet Black, and the Jessie Currie mentioned in the diary is possibly the child of this second marriage. Thomas Currie died in Scotland on 18 January 1870, aged seventy-five years.

Education Department, enclosing 'Mr Inglis promise'. July saw work in the garden planting carrots, cabbages, onions, shallots and four different kinds of peas. John planted the borders with strawberries and grapes. On 21 July he received a letter from the Education Department about land for the school, and went to Ingliston to organise the promised acre of land.

The work of the farm still came first, and it was hard and back-breaking work. On 22 August, John went with James to the forest to fell a tree. 'James not in good humour', he wrote, but added that they 'got 30 something posts'. The whole family helped with the work, and on 25 August John took Tom to Johnston's to clean oats, and noted, 'made 30 bags out of them'. There were frequent entries about the sale of oats, and their current price.

1.9   *Started for Ballarat with 14 Bags of Oats. Got up all right and came home next day got 5/2 for my load of oats.*

2.9   *Bought 6 Bags of Bone dust and a pair of chains. Got home by 10 o'clock sober.*

On 8 September John went to the Council meeting, 'wrote about the road the councillors decided to open it'. He also received a letter from the Hon. J. Casey enclosing a letter from the Land office dated 23 June 1872.

No doubt John was too tired by the end of the day to keep up his diary, and on 28 September 1873 a new hand recorded: 'John Currie has tired of keeping a Diary and has handed it over to me. C. Currie'. From this date the Currie story would be written by Catherine, who wrote in her book almost daily until her death more than three decades later. Whenever she was unable to write because of illness or child-birth, her husband and later her children would keep the record up to date. It became a chronicle of work completed, purchases made, produce sold. At times it became a place for confession, for stating the truths unable to be said directly to the other members of a family that did not indulge in much idle talk.

Idleness of any sort was anathema to the Curries. They prided themselves on their hard work, their decency and respectability. Their own dignity and independence was of vital importance to them, and occasionally Catherine noted that other people held rather too high an opinion of themselves. The Scottish background was important to the Curries, who still received letters and Scottish newspapers from their relatives in the Old Country. Catherine, who was not a Scot herself, had obviously picked up many of John's values and expressions.

7.11.73   *Mr. Thom called in the evening he is very meek indeed now so different from his first visits.*

9.11   *Went to church I and John to hear Mr. Thom, he does very well but he is a highland man.*

As a note of sarcasm, Catherine often finished an entry about someone else's idiosyncrasies with the ironical notation, 'ye ken'. Yet while maintaining their own dignity, sometimes at the expense of others, the Curries were usually tolerant of others' weaknesses. Sandy Grant was known to like a drink, and he often came to 'hinder the work', or to smash their plates at dinner time, but Catherine fed him and put up with him quite kindly. People's foibles could be tolerated if they did not threaten her own family. Indeed, maybe their peccadilloes threw the virtues of the Curries into higher relief.

Once Catherine began to keep the diary, there were more entries about her work, although John's work was still seen as the most vital contribution. On 1 October Catherine was carting bricks from the kiln and storing them in the barn to be ready for the building of a new dairy. Horses Dimple and Damsel carted the bricks while John was ploughing and harrowing. A week later James and Catherine went to cut some chaff at Grant's, and the next day helped to fence the wattles, to make a little stockyard, and to burn the stooks. On 13 October John planted some flowers, and then began to build the new dairy. John did a great deal of ploughing in October, while James and Catherine cut chaff and prepared loads of oats. The only respite was on Sunday; the minister had visited to ask the Curries to attend the service, and on most Sundays John and Catherine went together. Jane often went too, mainly so that she could walk home with Neil Cunningham.

In October and November the Curries began to reap the fruits of their labour. On 29 October John took seventeen bags of oats (76 bushels) to town, and sold them for 5s 5d per bushel. He was planting pumpkins, marrows, cucumbers, turnips and carrots, and in November began planting potatoes and maize. Oats were still selling at 5s 5d, and in November Catherine noted that the price of her butter had gone up a penny, and was now 7d per pound. On 26 November there was trouble selling the oats: 'there was a disturbance between the buyers and the Commission agents—it was not easy getting them sold'. The oats were eventually sold at 5s 3d per bushel. There were more complicated financial matters to worry about, and Catherine noted,

6.11   *Posted a letter to Scotland to Jessie Currie—received one from David Simpson—making complaints about Jessie Currie's affairs. John is very ill-pleased about it. Carrie came today she has left her place at Mrs Govetts Kyneton she is much thinner than she was when we saw her last.*

Catherine now had John's brother James, and her own sisters Jane and Carrie staying with her. Her father Leaper came often to visit, as did her brothers Ned and John. Neighbours visited all the time, seeking cuttings, asking to use Catherine's sewing machine, looking for advice about treatment for illnesses. For all their propinquity,

Catherine's women friends were rarely called by their first names, and sometimes made too many demands. On 4 December 1873 Catherine went to stay with Mrs Greenshields, Grant's housekeeper, when she gave birth to her daughter. She stayed for a week, and must have taken her diary with her, for she recorded that the Grants were cutting their rye-grass. Mr and Mrs Johnston brought Carrie over to visit, and Catherine learned that John was harrowing. She felt that she had been away from home too long, and called at Woodmuir on 7 December to find that John had picked the strawberries and was making jam himself. The next day she finally came home at midnight, and John brought her a plate of strawberries and cream in bed.

On 10 December John set off for Melbourne and returned the next day with tea, sugar, sago and raisins. He 'paid for the Crown Grant for our land did not get it home with him'. On 15 December a letter arrived from E. Steadman with a copy of Thomas Currie's will, and the next day Catherine was loading hay in the heat. Over the next few days she went to help the Johnstons bring in their hay. Brother Leaper arrived on 23 December, but on Christmas Eve Catherine noted 'Mr Wells junior made a great fuss and took himself off he has missed his Christmas Dinner'. Mr Wells senior arrived for Christmas dinner, and on 31 December brother Ned arrived to stay until 11 January. The Wells family visited often, but relationships seemed to be rather volatile.

1874

January 1874 was spent reaping wheat, and on 22 January the threshing machine arrived. The machine did the rounds of the district, and there was an occasional trauma when the machine broke down and parts were sent for urgently, sometimes from Melbourne. With the machine came men to help, and the Curries paid the men 3s 9d each for working for three-quarters of a day. On 20 January Catherine noted 'we went to Ballan—our lots of land on the hill were sold today—John bought them at upset prices'. The new block was on the side of Mount Darriwill, opposite their original selection, and the family would soon begin to build a house which had spectacular views over the selection. However, John was obviously on the look-out for new land in another district, and was talking with the Grants about the possibilities of Brandy Creek. On 24 January Catherine recorded, 'L. Grant here in the evening wants John to go with him to Brandy Creek on Monday'. It seems that nothing came of this suggestion, for John went on cutting his thistles. On 27 January the entry read, 'finished cutting our thistles—this is the day they are trying to evade the Thistle Act—with a Melbourne lawyer in Ballan'.

In February John was ploughing, and Catherine and Mrs Lynch went to rob the hives of bees that had been put in the blue gums and wattles. Both were stung by the angry bees, but they rubbed brandy on the stings and made mead from the honey. John sowed grass seed, and took three hams and a roll of bacon to sell to Ballan storekeeper Mr Flack. The hams brought 7s and the bacon was 9d per pound. The Curries earned a total of £2 10s 3d. In the next weeks Catherine helped with the harrowing, and took another fifty pounds of ham to Mr Flack.

On 1 March the Curries went to the Grants to see when they were going to Brandy Creek. Catherine noted, 'they think Lack will start on Wednesday but will let us know on Tuesday'. When John had not heard from Lachlan, he set out alone for Brandy Creek on 4 March, but Catherine recorded that 'L. Grant passed just after John—with spring cart and dray with rye grass'. John came home again on 15 March, arriving after the family had gone to bed, and bringing some Brandy Creek sticks and some cucumbers. He had pegged out some land, but Catherine did not confide his impressions of Gippsland to her diary. On 17 April two letters arrived from E. B. Steadman, with details of the death of John's father. In May the Curries sold bacon and eggs to Mr Flack, receiving 9d per pound for the bacon and 2s a dozen for the eggs. On 23 May, 'John went to Ballarat—got the Deeds for his land—both pieces—but did not get Thomas Bryces—or James Currie —should have taken an order for them from us'.

It seems that John was preparing information about his Ballan land in order to select land at Lardner's Track. On 8 June a letter came from Ballarat 'about James Crown Grant'. Through July Catherine went on making and selling her butter, selling eight pounds at 11d per pound on 14 July, and just six pounds for 1s on 20 July. John planted peas, potatoes, onions, parsley and cress, and carted firewood. On the last day of the month, Catherine noted that there were twenty-four new lambs. Despite the continuing work of the farm, and his plans for building a house on the new block, John seemed set on moving to a new selection. On 2 August he saw Lach Grant, who had just come home from Brandy Creek, and on 4 August he set off again 'to meet the surveyor'. For Catherine, surrounded by sister, children and neighbours, life seemed very lonely without him there, and there was no one else who could provide such good material for her diary.

5.8 *John is not here for me to write what he is at work doing so I must say what I did myself . . . I am very lonely.*

9.8 *Sunday is a lonely day without John. I wish he was here.*

John came home again on 13 August with the news that some one else had claimed the land he had pegged in March. He wrote a few letters, and on 30 September 'John got a letter from Surveyor W. Thornhill saying send him £28 8s, and a filled up form to Mr Callanan at Gipps Land. Took James to Ballan but could not get a Magistrate so returned.'

The next day Catherine noted that there were serious decisions to be made:

1.10   *What shall we do about this land—John does not know—I see he is set on trying for it—so what can I do but advise him to go—they must go and peg it out again. What has been done goes for nothing. He is not going to get it all in James name this time. I am so glad of that—one should not trust too much in others.*

2.10   *John started this morning for Gippsland James with him—I could very well have asked John not to go at all—but what would he do he must go looking for it sometime as it will not come to no one— I feel so miserable. I do hope he will get on well but John is so shy among folks that he does not like to go so far away from home.*

On 9 October John arrived home, having managed 'first rate'. He had pegged out 110 acres for himself, and an adjoining block of 320 acres for James. On 12 November, the diary recorded, 'Got the deeds for the Land on the Hill this time'. In the same month John began to build the new house, and Catherine helped him, worrying about him almost obsessively, sometimes to her own detriment.

25.11   *Started to put the roof on the house the wall plate fell down on my head—it gave me a good knock—but was not so bad as it might have been—I was so glad that it fell on me instead of John.*

Catherine worked as hard as John, although there was some division of labour. John did the heavy fieldwork, but Catherine helped by harrowing and filling in crab-holes, and with the never-ending task of thistle cutting. In November 1874 they began to shear the small flock of sheep. After a while the shears refused to function, so Catherine took up her scissors to finish the job. She had to admit defeat with only five sheep to go.

1875

In January John and Catherine were pulling hemp, with Tom and Katie helping. One morning they all got up at 3 a.m. so that they could finish their work by ten o'clock and so avoid the searing heat of the day. Catherine noted that oats, selling in December for 5s per bushel, were now selling for 4s 4d, and on 28 January that they had threshed 150 bags of oats, 'paid £5 for thrashing and £1 18s for men and bullocks'. In February the diary recorded that 140 bags of oats had been sold for £113 19s.

As well as oats, the family sold wheat, hay, wool and bacon, and surplus horses, sheep and cattle. Much of the family's food was produced on the farm: meat, vegetables, fruit, milk, butter, honey and eggs were the basis of their ample diet. From the vegetable garden came carrots, cabbages, turnips, artichokes, onions, shallots, pumpkins, marrows, cucumbers, lettuces, radishes and strawberries, and the orchard produced apples, pears and plums. Catherine earned a regular income selling eggs and butter, and she spent the money she earned on materials for clothes, sugar, coffee, tea, flour, gin and brandy for medicinal purposes and for Sandy Grant, books for the children, boots, the *Age* and the *Leader*. She sometimes grumbled about 'how quick money slips away', but she had money of her own from butter-making, and she felt able to buy eau-de-cologne or a shawl costing £2 5s at a bazaar in Ballan. Salesmen came to her door, but the most important caller was the butterman, who came weekly. He took the six or seven pounds of butter she had made during the week, as well as eggs. Catherine bought five or six pounds of sugar from him each week, and sometimes coffee or a bucket or a pie dish. In weeks when she made several purchases it is probable that no money changed hands as she bartered her butter for items she needed.

Men helped each other with machinery and labour during harvest, sometimes without being asked. The touchy and self-reliant Curries were not always pleased, and Catherine noted when the Brennans came to help, 'We would rather they had not come but could not send them away when they did' [Jan 75]. The Curries were careful not to be too dependent on others, and to make sure they were not imposed upon. When John broke the plough and a neighbour offered to lend him one, 'he took it for a wonder' [27.4.74]. Catherine grumbled that 'Old Sutherland came up and took a load of straw without leave—just like his impudence' [29.1.75], and she made a record in her diary of all the goods she had lent, as neighbours could not always be trusted. On 8 May 1874 she noted:

> *I went to see Grant's housekeeper gave me the Tea that she borrowed from me at Christmas time—she had lost the bag I sent it in and I am sure that I did not get near as much as I sent—I should have weighed it before I gave it.*

It was easier to give away things that cost no money, and Catherine was generous with cuttings from her garden and orchard. There were massive exchanges of seeds, cuttings and fruit graftings, and in this way European plants colonised large areas of Victoria. Catherine Currie was a keen gardener, and her cuttings added to the orchards and gardens of many of her neighbours.

In February of 1875 John went to Melbourne, where the Gippsland land was 'recommended to him'. On the day he got home, a Valentine card came for him, addressed to John Currie, Ballan; 'surely a mistake', Catherine decided. In March John set off again for his new property, and Catherine worried about him as usual. Frequent letters passed between them, but Catherine was not reassured.

20.3.75 *Oh dear I know he is not well by the way he writes—what shall I do—I would go to him if I knew the way from Whiskey Creek*

The next day she spent 'nearly all day writing to John', but on 23 March she got a happier letter, and two days later John returned safely. On 31 March he started once more for Gippsland with Lachlan Grant. Catherine was again lonely among the crowd.

31.3 *John went away again this morning—and I am so lonely—although Lizzie is here too—but I think no one any company but John.*

4.4 *Nobody here yet nor Jane neither—plenty of folks came last Sunday—when I wanted John all to myself—no one today to keep me from worrying.*

By 15 April Catherine had received a letter to say that John had moved into his new hut. She wrote, 'would like it fine if we were with him—wish we were'. The next day a buyer paid Catherine £5 for some hay, and she remarked 'I was *very* glad to get it—as I was quite out of funds —how quick money slips away—I can hardly reckon on it as it goes in shillings or two'. John arrived home again on 24 May and began to take berry cuttings for the new farm. On 3 July Catherine, who had recorded a month before that she had been out trying to lift a cow, gave birth to a son, described by his father as a 'perfect man'. John went away again on 21 July, leaving Jane to register the new baby as Albert Bryce.

On 4 September Sandy Grant was very ill with enlargement of the liver, and on 8 September John returned home for the last time, far from well himself. On 30 September Catherine recorded, 'Sandy Grant here making arrangements to buy the farm'; meaning it, happily, literally and not figuratively. On 7 October 1875, 'John met Mr. Grant at Mr. Musgraves and settled about the ground. I hardly know the terms yet but it is £5 per acre'.

20.10.75 *John went to Ballan to advertise this Place on the Hill, gave it into Welsh's hands, the auctioneers.*

21.10.75 *John got a note from Musgrave to say that he had paid Mr. Grant's cheque into the Bank for three hundred pounds, £300 to our credit, and his bill for £283 for collection due 10th April 1877. Sarah Cowan, Mr. Grant's housekeeper here and bought this place from me for the sum of £50.*

A week later Catherine wrote, 'got the place transferred to Sarah Cowen. She has not got an answer to her letter about the money yet'. The next few days passed in a flurry of business transactions, in shopping trips and visits from neighbours. At the end of October 'John put £200 to interest bearing 5 per cent. That is more than I thought they gave'.

The Curries planned to leave Ballan on the first day of November but for two days it was too wet to begin. The next day John started for Bacchus Marsh with the sheep. Meanwhile neighbours gave Catherine and the children bread, 'as we are all eaten up'. John returned the following day with a tarpaulin to protect their belongings and on 5 November Catherine's father brought his cart, loaded all they were to take with them, and the journey began. Sunday was spent resting with Catherine's parents in Bacchus Marsh; neither Catherine nor John was feeling well but Catherine did visit some old friends.

The following day they readied themselves and their horses, Doctor and Dimple, to journey once more, but wild weather held them up for three days. Finally, on 11 November, *we made a start and bid goodbye to the Marsh—fine day, rather warm—poor old Doctor knocked up just at Deep Creek—we had to leave him—we camped at the new powder magazine—fine night liked it fine—about 9 o'clock PM when we stopt fine and moonlight.*

Next day they reached Melbourne about eleven o'clock, met Catherine's brother and sister and went to the photographers with the baby.

12.11.75 *Met Lizzie and Ned there got one likeness taken—but baby was not good—the little rogue—he was never bad before but he got a nasty fall this morning—and it was so hot there—he was just taken asleep—we left Melbourne about 4 o'clock and camped again about Oakleigh fine night.*

13.11.75 *Started about 9 this morning and got on fast John says—camped again at Pakenham all good roads as yet—saw some notices on the trees at Dandenong about the Scarlet Fever—frightened me a bit—but it was only the Crs. cautioning folks (at the ratepayers expense) to be careful as it was spreading in Melbourne.*

After another day's journey they were bogged in the Bishop's swamp. They camped where they stopped and the next morning unloaded the cart and pushed it out. After getting stuck once more at the Bunyip Creek they camped all night on the hillside above Whisky Creek. Catherine was tired, and slept soundly and 'never heard the Gipps Land coach pass within a couple of feet of us—and I wanted so much to see it'.

On 16 November a new neighbour, Charles Harkness, lent them his horse to pull them through from Whisky Creek to Kelvin Grove, and then they stopped again for Catherine to visit Mrs Greenshields and her baby who had already moved to a new selection from Bacchus Marsh. Here Catherine discovered the reason for Bert's irritability at the Melbourne photographers. A thread of his stocking had been caught between his toes, cutting him. On 17 November Lachlan Grant and McPherson and his son helped John to cut a track through the dense scrub to their new block. Catherine recorded, 'Started after dinner time—got over safe—very rough road I thought—it was just what Dimple could do to bring us'. Neighbours came to offer milk and meat, and a tree was felled across the swamp so that Catherine could visit her closest neighbour, Mrs Hardie.

22.11.75 *Katie with me and Baby—I like them very well—for a first visit they said it was quite an event my going—as I was the first Lady visitor they had had.*

The next day John negotiated with Walter McKay, an old Ballan neighbour, to saw timber for the new house. He decided on a site for the dwelling and Catherine thought it 'a splendid place for a home like it fine'.

At the end of 1875 a letter came to say that Catherine's sister Jane had married Neil Cunningham, who had selected a block of land close by. On the last day of the year John posted a letter to the government acknowledging the receipt of licences for James Currie's block. The die had been cast for many of the Ballan community, who were now moving together into the wilderness. For the moment, 30-year-old Catherine Currie sat in her small wooden hut surrounded by three small children and the towering eucalypts and dense undergrowth of the Gippsland forest. This was a very different environment from the one she had left, but she saw it as a new and hopeful beginning, and she liked it fine.

Selection

Even before the island continent had been searched and mapped horizontally from sea to sea, the search began for the treasures hidden beneath the surface. In 1858 Leaper Hurry Wells and John Currie were digging deep and vertical holes into the Australian soil, searching for the golden substance described prosaically as a 'precious yellow non-rusting malleable ductile metal of high specific gravity'.[9] The scientific description hid the deep symbolism of gold: a short and beautiful four-lettered word that conjured up dreams of wealth and poetry.

In the same year, 1858, two men back in the home country unearthed a different kind of treasure. Alfred Wallace and Charles Darwin had independently and simultaneously produced the theory of natural selection. Based on a study of the natural world (part of it in Australia), the theory said that evolution occurs because those members of a species whose characteristics best fit them for survival are those that contribute most offspring to the next generation. In this way the adaptation of the species to its environment will gradually be improved. The name of natural selection also hid a deep symbolism: this theory would change the map of human thought and alter the narrative of progress.[10]

No doubt Catherine Currie knew little about the new theory of natural selection, and would not have considered it of personal interest if she had. With hindsight, we may think of her as living on the edge of an ambiguity, a shift in thinking which would soon have to consider the possibility that the world could be formed by accident rather than by design. At first it appeared that the theory might reinforce the idea of a narrative of progress, of taxonomies of time as well as of species. Family trees would merely have to be extended back a few million years; the end of the stor y was apparent, but the beginning was now to be altered.

But the survival of the fittest, says the theory, occurs through non-adaptive mutations, or chance. In *Chance and Necessity*, Jacques Monod says that one of the characteristics of living beings is that they are capable of faithfully reproducing themselves—they have an 'accuracy of translation' that makes the organism conservative, stable and resist-ant to change. But the fidelity of translation is not absolute, and once a mistake is made it is irreversible. Every now and then there are minute errors of transcription, and these can never be corrected. Such accidents are 'essentially unpredictable because always singular'.[11] There lurks here always an unpredictable element which may change the end of the story.

The narrative Catherine was writing was a singular narrative, and the fact of its existence has selected her for scrutiny as the singular sub-ject. She indeed considered herself to be selected, one of the chosen few who would create a new civilisation in the wilderness. While the general laws of the universe concerned the species and not the individ-ual, the rule of the narrative decreed that the author would be the mid-point. The idea of accident and chance was not popular in the nineteenth century, particularly not with families such as the Curries, whose ideas of responsibility and obligation were instilled into them by culture, religion and society. The survival of the fittest was linked to the ethic of hard work and independence, and the accuracy of translation from one society to another was only mediated by self-determination and a conscious choice.

While the Curries may or may not have heard of natural selection, they well knew the importance of a different sort of selection which had been the talk of the colonies since the mid 1850s. This subject was the divisive staple of political debate from the time they arrived in Australia, and people defined their political views around the issue. The Curries knew that the selection of land was a choice that could bring them wealth and happiness and give them opportunities in the new country that an accident of birth would have denied them in the old. This was an example of choice and self-determination at its finest.

By the beginning of the 1870s thousands of people had pegged out their new land and had began to clear and farm it; in the year of 1874 alone over eleven thousand selections had been claimed. Much of the best land close to Melbourne and in the Western District had already fallen into private hands as a result of earlier Selection Acts and other land legislation. This legislation allowed selection only in areas already chosen and surveyed by the government, and it was under the earlier selection acts that John Currie had taken up his land at Ballan.

Natural selection highlights the need for adaptation, and the inhabitants of a rapidly depleting goldfield now sought to turn themselves into a stable community of yeoman farmers. While animals will unconsciously adapt to conditions over millions of years, the human animal is blessed or cursed with the gift of memory as well as of prediction. Steering themselves towards a future filled with prosperous and contented farmers, the migrants from the United Kingdom were also seeking in their own way to re-create the bucolic ideal that had been shattered in the old country as a result of the industrial revolution.

The Grant Act of 1869 opened up to selection before survey most Victorian land that was not already in private hands. The intending selector could choose up to 320 acres of land, peg out its boundaries, arrange to have it surveyed, and then apply to the Lands Department for the block. If successful, the selector held the land under licence from the Crown for three years. During this time he or she had to improve the land by building a house and boundary fences, and by clearing and cultivating a tenth of the acreage selected. If these conditions were met and the annual rental of a shilling an acre was paid, a lease was granted. Payment of the same rent for a further seven years (amounting to a total payment of £1 per acre over ten years) gave the selector freehold title to the land.[12]

The new Act sparked a rush into the Wimmera, the Goulburn Valley and the northern counties. Some of those who joined the land rush had never farmed before, but many had already tilled the soil south of the Divide. They sold out to their neighbours, intending to use the capital from their first, now tired selections, on larger blocks further north.

By 1873 neighbours of John Currie were considering moving south into Gippsland rather than north into the Wimmera or the Goulburn Valley. The task of clearing the forested land was obviously more formidable, but the intending selector had a wider choice of land with fewer people competing for it. In 1873 the surveyor for the Lands Department, John Lardner, drove a track from the Old Sale Road at Brandy Creek due south to the survey line for the proposed rail link from Melbourne through to Sale. Lardner's Track was bounded on each side by farmable land; intending selectors promptly flowed along the track and within three years all the useable land had been selected. Lachlan Grant selected at Lang Warry in the early part of 1873, but still maintained 140 acres of grazing land in Ballan. As John and his brother James began taking trips to Gippsland in search of suitable land, other neighbours such as Thomas Greenshields, Thomas Booker and Walter McKay were doing the same.

The Australian version of natural selection, the survival of the fittest, saw the selector as the independent, hard-working and self-reliant battler who fought for democracy and decency, a small green plot and the future of his own smiling children. It was a variation of a myth that grew from all newly settled countries, but it had its own Australian flavour. In North America, the first settlers fought dourly to turn the coastal forests into small productive farms, before others ventured inland to the larger and wilder adventure of the open plains. In Australia the first major protagonists and heroes were the big men, the explorers who discovered the open country, and the large pastoralists who stocked it. Only later did the story extend to the battle of the small man to carve out a place for himself and his family on smaller plots.

The settler myth was about the rights of every man to a 'fair go', an equal chance, a right to the land and status he could never hope to gain in the old world. It was also about progress and civilisation and the imposition of 'the normal'. It was the small farmer who would tame this wild land, fence off small plots in order to build his cottage and plant his crops and garden. Speaking of the similar rural myth of New Zealand, Miles Fairbairn describes the common view of the frontier as 'nature's untamed wilderness which feeds the beast in men'. He notes, 'By comparison, cultivated and domesticated nature was seen as a conception of nature as Eden, of apple orchards and vineyards, of children playing in thick-leaved trees, and singing mothers'.[13]

Coral Lansbury suggests that the Australian legend grew partly from English writers who were disillusioned with their own post-industrial reality, and who saw Australia as a new Arcadia. The legend, she says, was as much the result of this mythology of Australia in English literature as it was an expression of experience:

The egalitarian, Arcadian expression of Australia was composed not in the nineties in the bush of Australia, but in England during the fifties by Sidney, Dickens and Lytton. The sardonic mockery of Australian writers like Henry Lawson and Joseph Furphy was the reaction of experience in Australia itself to the English literary imagination.[14]

Catherine Currie began to write her diary before Henry Lawson or Joseph Furphy had 'reacted to experience'. She was a selector's wife before Lawson or Barbara Baynton wrote their stories, she had buried a baby in a bush cemetery before Frederick McCubbin painted his portrait of the Pioneers. She was not a creation of myth, and she had not heard that she should be cowed and oppressed by the vastness of the land or the silences of her quiet husband. She was a young woman of firm opinions and strong convictions, eager, despite some misgivings, for the new adventure at the last frontier.

The civilising of nature, says Fairbairn, was a family affair. The idyllic home in the forest was run by a mother who loved the finer things of life, appreciated the beauty of flowers and music, and brought order to her environment inside and outside the home. There was a slight danger that such a woman would tip the balance from refinement to 'fussiness', towards that artificial culture that is more at home in the city, and does not sit well with the beauty of the tamed and ordered natural world. But this myth was solidly based on the family.[15]

The governments of the day were strongly in favour of this civilising and family ideal, and the making of money from the sale of unused land was hidden beneath this rhetoric. In the South Australian parliament it had been claimed in 1875 that, as the result of opening land for selection,

the country would be . . . covered with smiling homesteads and prosperous farms . . . and that the land would be held by a numerous population enjoying that state of existence described in the Scriptures as neither poverty nor riches, the soil being held and tilled by a yeomanry, who would be a moral, religious, upright community spreading happiness around them.[16]

There is no explicit discussion in the diary of the reasons for the Curries' move to Gippsland, although throughout 1873 there are entries about Lachlan Grant's comings and goings to Brandy Creek, and many neighbours were interested in and talking about the new land. Maybe once one had decided to go the others were afraid they might miss out on this last chance to select. It seems that John was the instigator of the Currie move. Catherine noted that he had his mind set on it, and she felt that she could do nothing but encourage him to go ahead, although she did worry if this was the right course.

John had decided that his property at Ballan was becoming too small, and he was thinking of his growing family and the need to provide for them in the years to come. He may also have noticed that, despite the good rainfall of 1873, his land was less productive than it had been. Many selections south of the Divide had been cropped for upwards of a decade, usually without adequate manuring to replenish nutrients drawn out by the crops, and the soils were becoming exhausted. The local council's decision to build a road through the Currie property was another problem; although John vigorously objected to the decision, he was unable to change it. These were good and concrete reasons to justify a move, circumstances that contributed to John's decision. It was not by chance that John Currie had become an immigrant, and it was by similar reasoned choice and conscious determination that he would select himself and his family as pioneers.

After several trips to Gippsland John and James decided to select land at Brandy Creek, and pegged out a block in the name of James Currie. They were guided by Lachlan and Sandy Grant, who already knew the area; John was fortunate in being able to rely on friends rather than local 'experts' who demanded payment but did not always direct land seekers to good land.[17] But the surveyor moved slowly; they lost this first selection to others.

At the time John was quite happy with his second selection of October 1874 and Catherine recorded in her diary,

9.10.74   *Managed first rate. Pegged again 400 and 30 acres I think. John is in great spirits and very glad he went.*

Four months went by before John and James were asked 'to attend Land Board at Melbourne' [9.2.74]. John was temporarily delayed by illness but returned triumphant after appearing before the Board: 'Got on first rate the land recommended to them', said Catherine four days later. James had selected 320 acres and John 110; as he had already selected over 200 acres many years earlier at Ballan, this was all he could ask for to make a total of 320 acres allowable under the Grant Act. It seems that the brothers intended running the property jointly as a family concern, and by realising James's 'selection potential', John had increased his holding to 430 acres.

James's selection was confirmed without a hitch but the Lands Department was suspicious of John and wanted to know what had happened to his previous selection. Two months went by and in desperation John wrote to Peter Lalor, his parliamentary representative:

Sir,

  As one of your representatives I ask your advice having in October last applied for a piece of land and made the necessary declarations. It was on the 12th of February recommended at Melbourne Local Land Board, the gentlemen forming the board informed me that I would get an order to occupy in about seven days. Sometime in May I received a letter from the Department enquiring about a former selection I made. Now in my declaration I mentioned that and only selected this piece to make up 320 acres.

I then asked to be informed about my being so long kept wait-ing and was told that they had some doubts about my Bonafides and that the district surveyor was making enquiries. The first piece 80 acres I selected in 1865 was so poor a piece I was going to forfeit only one of my neighbours said he would pay my expenses if I transferred to him. I did with the authority of the Board of Land. The other piece I still live on but as it is ten years since I occupied it is getting too small now. I have called several times and get for answer that I will get an answer in a few days it makes me heart-sick if they would refuse. I could go to NSW or some other place but they keep my money and me waiting now as this is a scrubby country if I do not get it now it will be no use for another year as it must be cut and burned before it is any use.

I must apologise for troubling you with my personal affair but I am not acquaint with anyone who is capable of advising me what to do to push them to give me an answer yes or no.

I remain dear Sir,
Yours to Command,
John Currie[18]

This appeal had the desired effect for within three weeks John was being asked to pay the first instalment of rent on his new selection.

Once they settled in Gippsland, the Curries were among old friends. Lachlan Grant had acted as the leader for the district, and had provided vital information about the availability of land, the fertility of soils and the whereabouts of water. He also gave directions for finding the new spot with the result that old neighbours selected close to each other in new locations and thus formed the nucleus of a new farming community. Walter McKay had taken up the block next to James, and the McPhersons, the Greenshields, the Murdies and Duncan Rose were all from Ballan.

There was a complicated network of friends and kin. The Curries' closest neighbours were Joseph and Agnes Hardie. They had come from Melbourne, where Joseph had worked as an engineer, but there was a Bacchus Marsh connection. Joseph was a cousin of Ninian Hardie, who had come from the Pentland Hills area at the same time as Lachlan Grant. Ninian pegged his 320-acre Springwood Park in 1873, and the next year Joseph arrived to peg 640 acres opposite the land that would become the Currie selection on Lardner's Track. Half was in Joseph Hardie's name and half in the name of his wife's sister, Elizabeth Broad. The house and land at Broadwood would become the property of Joseph Hardie when Elizabeth died in 1877.

The Grants also brought other family members. Lachlan was one of the first settlers on Lardner's Track, and Sandy, although he stayed in the Bacchus Marsh area, also selected. George Grant, who was later to be an influential member of the community, was married to Sandy's sister Jessie, and had a successful business as a manufacturer of farming implements in Melbourne. George rented a grazing property at Pentland Hills, which he shared with other members of the Grant family. He followed his relations to Brandy Creek, and his wife inherited Sandy's selection, Glenfern, in the area.[19] In February 1877 the Bairds, relations of Catherine's family, arrived from the Marsh to select close by.

The hilly forest country along Lardner's Track was very different from the flat, cleared uplands that John had farmed at Ballan. The prevailing view was that massive scrub growth indicated high soil fertility, yet the people who rushed to peg out the Gippsland forests must have had vivid imaginations to see green pastures through the trees, and stout hearts to contemplate the clearing effort that would be required. As with so many migrations, a spirit of group euphoria may have obscured some harsh realities. William Salmon, another Buln Buln selector noted

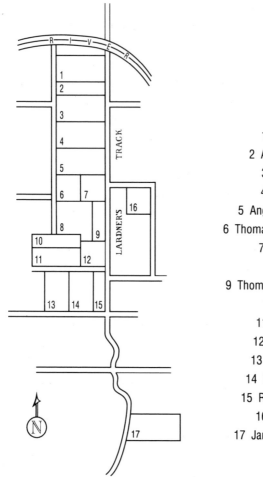

1 George Grant (320 acres)

2 Alexander Grant (160 acres)

3 Duncan Rose (320 acres)

4 Ninian Hardie (320 acres)

5 Angus McPherson (320 acres)

6 Thomas Greenshields (164 acres)

7 Lachlan Grant (160 acres)

8 John Syme (305 acres)

9 Thomas Collingwood (110 acres)

10 John Currie (110 acres)

11 James Currie (320 acres)

12 Walter McKay (134 acres)

13 Joseph Hardie (320 acres)

14 Elizabeth Broad (320 acres)

15 Robert Hamilton (106 acres)

16 M. McMurdie (320 acres)

17 Jane Cunningham (320 acres)

Selections along Lardner's Track. This stylised drawing is not to scale but shows the relative positions of the neighbours along the track. The track ran due south from Brandy Creek, and would become the boundary between the parishes of Drouin to the west and Warragul to the east. The reserve for the railway line to Melbourne ran to the north of George Grant's property.

many thousands ... are being enticed here by the luxuriant appearance of the vegetation and the beauties of the forest, and last but not least by the sanguine articles that often appear in the public papers ... So many have, and are, throwing up fine situations and paying businesses in order to obtain 320 acres of land, and in the majority of cases, with the idea that, by an expenditure of £1 to £300, they can in a year or two earn a good living. Naturally, they find it difficult or impossible to, at order, transform a forest into a paying farm, and so they are disenchanted ...[20]

Yet in 1875 Catherine sat in her new hut in the forest and 'liked it fine'. This was the beginning of a new adventure that promised wealth and happiness. The child of gold-rush parents, Catherine understood the search for new opportunities and a secure future for her children. Land was a four-letter word just as valuable as gold, and probably more respectable. Selectors were those self-reliant, decent and hardworking people who were conscious of their status as pioneers and owners of land. But the move was also a gamble, a search for material well-being. It was a chance to rise in the hierarchy of society by becoming larger landholders, and it was fuelled by a desperation not to be left behind on inferior properties while neighbours were moving to richer land. This would be survival of the fittest and now, in the human progression, of the most determined.

The move to the forest took the Curries from the undulating gold plains of Ballan to the deep green of a giant forest which had been formed by natural selection over millions of years. It was a forest teeming with animal, bird and plant life, but until opened for selection it had been literally, in white terms, a No Man's Land and definitely a No Woman's Land. Into this missing paragraph of European history would be projected the rhetoric of the pioneer, and the deliberate adaptation of an environment to human need and continuity.

The theory of natural selection says that each person has successful ancestors. 'We all, without a single exception, inherit all our genes from an unbroken line of successful ancestors.'[21] Success is measured by the fact that each ancestor has survived to childbearing age, and has managed to find a mate. But the human species has ensured that the 'accuracy of translation' has been changed by determination and free will; by conscious choices as well as accidental mutations.

Catherine Currie had been brought to Australia at the age of seven, a choice made for her by her parents. She had married John at the age of nineteen, and according to the conventions of her time she followed him wherever he chose to go—although, the diary tells us, not without some words and thoughts of her own. It was her own choice to write about her life, and this is the reason that she has been selected for contemplation. Our choice to turn her autobiography into biography has made her representative as well as singular, for as the biographer James F. Veninga says,

> Through biography we gain knowledge of the universal conditions under which all lives are formed and lived, the conditions of freedom and fate. By fate I mean the limits of circumstance, the conditions of a person's life that can be affirmed or transcended only by choice.[22]

In Catherine's case, the limits of circumstance could not always be transcended by choice, and it is only after the fact that we may dig beneath the surface of the narrative to seek the variations of chance and necessity.

The modern thinker Michel Foucault has used the word 'archaeology' to denote 'the history of that which renders necessary a certain form of thought'.[23] He moved from the linear and horizontal account of progress to those vertical layers of thought which exist beneath the surface. Only the uncovering of these layers would illustrate how concepts and ideas had been laid down over centuries. Just as mineral or vegetable matter may be pressed by time and immense natural forces to turn into diamond or coal or oil, so ways of thinking can be altered by structural and cultural forces.

The map and the story of human evolution has another dimension, a vertical as well as a horizontal aspect. The signifying chain by which the unique experience of the individual is constituted, says Foucault, is 'perpendicular to the formal system on the basis of which the significations of a culture are constituted':

> at any given instant, the structure proper to individual experience finds a certain number of possible choices (and of excluded possibilities) in the systems of the society; inversely, at each of their points of choice the social structures encounter a certain number of possible individuals (and others who are not)—just as the linear structure of language always produces a possible choice between several words or several phonemes at any given moment (but excludes all others).[24]

Catherine was under the impression that she had a choice about her life and the manner in which it was lived, and all her decisions were made on this assumption. The words of her diary set the boundaries of her experiences, and perhaps it seemed to her that the leather covers of her books would enclose the story of a life without ambiguity or digression. Yet every choice of word or experience excluded another, and many choices were in fact denied to her by virtue of time and place, gender and circumstance. Naturally selected as a subject by virtue of her written words, she now becomes object in our examination of her words. As we transcribe her words into the slightly different grammar and form demanded by our time and place, we seek the archaeology, the layer beneath the surface, the mistake in the transcription that will alter the narrative.

Lardner 1876–1879

1876

The new year, like the new life, began with hope and happiness. On New Year's Day there was a picnic given by the Bachelors of Lardner's Track, and Catherine recorded, 'it was a most enjoyable affair—we were all quite pleased with it—got home in good time'. Such qualified approval was high praise from Catherine. The next day the Curries went on a 'ramble' with their new neighbours the Hardies, and Catherine was in fine form.

> *Met Mr. O'Mahoney coming Back—such a cure—he says he gets an average of 16 papers a week—and he thinks he is the Coming Man of Buln Buln.*

The next day John and Catherine each killed a snake, and a splitter came to take wood to cut for the new home—'8s per hundred for palings and £2 per 1000 for shingles'. McKay came to help John cut saplings, and to make a pathway wide enough to transport saplings to 'the house place'.

These first months were very busy, even by the high standards of the Curries. The new farm was in the middle of almost impenetrable bush and John had to clear constantly just to keep the track into the farm open. He cleared the space for the new house by burning, at first without much success. Between preparing the site and materials for the new house he sowed potatoes, shallots and turnips, and the whole family killed snakes. By 16 January they had accounted for twelve. On 24 January, Catherine recorded, 'John went to bring the shingles—had to pack them to Grants fence—them splitters wants kicking for getting them so far away—very Hot'. By 27 January John had paid £10 for the shingles, although he was not pleased with them, and on 5 February he started to build the house.

So far, there was no money coming in from the new farm, but on 12 February John received a letter from Sandy Grant with a cheque for £5 12s, 'being price of our wool 150 lbs at 9d per lb.' The money must have been a help. Catherine was still wondering at her new home. The snakes may not have been welcome visitors, but there were other animals and birds: on 14 February she noted, 'such a great Hawk here this morning'. McKay came to help erect the wall plates for the house; at the end of the month Hardie came to put in the windows, 'John waiting on him and sawing Boards for Battens between while thats hard work for I tried it yesterday'.

In March John went to Melbourne for supplies of flour, salt, sugar, tea, oatmeal and dried apples. He also bought some barley, which he sowed in one of his cleared paddocks. The shingling was finished, and now he was putting in the floor, although there was no chimney yet. On 22 March, Catherine noted, 'washed up at the House today. James carried the water James had a pain in his chest I gave him some whiskey it cured it'. On 27 March John started for town again, leaving James and Catherine sowing barley. On 3 April John returned, bringing Jane, as well as ten bags of rye-grass, two of cocksfoot, one hundred pounds of clover, flour, four chairs, a case of kerosene and some pans and kettles. In spite of all the work, the Curries visited the Grants or the Hardies nearly every day, and had constant visitors at Brandie Braes. On 8 April John sowed the grasses he had bought, and they received a bill from the seed merchant for £46 19s 6d: 'what a lot of money just for seed—and nearly as much last time for groceries', recorded Catherine.

On his visits to Melbourne for supplies John was often accompanied by neighbours, and the settlers assisted each other as much as they could. Catherine gave Mrs Hardie lessons on the sewing machine, and John went to a public meeting to see if the selectors wished to form a shire. On 5 April John went to clear out Grant's shed for a school. Thomas Collingwood, a neighbouring selector, was to be the first teacher. The same building was used for religious services every Sunday afternoon, and soon became the meeting place for old and new friends. Thomas Collingwood, Joseph Hardie or John Currie would give the sermon; they asked for other volunteers, but no one came forward. The Greenshields and the McEvoys, neighbours from Ballan, arrived to peg land for Ned McEvoy, and Jane came again in April to see the block her new husband, Neil Cunningham, had pegged out. Jane went home on 19 April, and Neil arrived in June to cut scrub on his selection.

On 1 May the children started at their new school. There was some trouble with a neighbour when Murdie's cattle strayed; John gave him 'a great blowing up', and told him not to let his animals wander over Currie land without permission. John was clearing and fencing, and 'he made a great fire', planted wheat and continued building the house. News came from the Hardies that Miss Broad had gone to see the doctor in Melbourne, and they were afraid that she had cancer. On 5 June Catherine went to visit Mrs Hardie, who was very ill. John continued clearing, with the help of McKay.

13.6 *John measuring and settling with McKay for ringing and cutting*
75¼ acres of land at 12/– per acre gave him cheque for £21.17s he
got £24.16s in grasses and other seeds with some cash.

June was cold and wet. Neil arrived and helped John with some of
his heavier work, and in return John went with him to his new block
to clear a place for the hut. McKay began to ringbark twenty acres
around the Currie house while John ploughed and cleared, and
plastered the walls of the house with mud. He began to build a
chimney, gardened and planted oats. It seemed that the new life would
mirror the old, even to the odd eccentric visitor. Mr Syme arrived on
29 June to have tea with the Curries; he had selected a block next door.
The following day Catherine recorded, 'Mr Syme the Pentridge
Turnkey came for John to help him choose a site for hut'. In July John
had finished sowing his rye paddock and cleared and fenced a
paddock for the oats. He was still carting and clearing, ploughing and
raking, and in August he planted two acres of oats. On 8 August the
Murdie cattle caused more consternation when they got into the barley
—'have now taken it every straw', said Catherine. Mr O'Mahoney
came 'to present Sir C. G. Duffy campaign to John'. O'Mahoney was
considering entering politics himself.
    According to Catherine, the Curries were already becoming the
local arbiters of taste and judgement. In August Catherine and John
went for a walk to see G. J. Walsh's house and garden. Jack Walsh was
an old neighbour from Ballan, but his property 'is very poor John
thinks', Catherine noted. On 24 September Catherine put pen to
paper to complain in a letter to the *Leader* about the Murdie cattle that
could not be kept out of their paddocks. The Curries were taking their
place as responsible members of the community. While John took his
turn giving the sermon, James sang at the church services. McKay,
who could not write, often came to ask Catherine to write a letter

home for him, and when young Betty and Joe Hardie became ill, the Curries visited solicitously. When the butcher came on 13 September with 166 pounds of beef, they paid him £3 2s 3d, and took twenty pounds to the Hardies. They also handed out good but stern advice; in October Joseph Hardy was complaining about his children, for Joe had gone home from the Curries without his hat, despite constant reminders. 'John told him he had better have whipped him and sent him back himself', said Catherine.

By the first Lardner spring of 1876, the family was housed in basic accommodation, had a small vegetable garden and some horses, sheep, dogs, pigs and poultry. Catherine noted laconically nearly every day, 'John clearing'. On 7 September the Curries 'filled up the paper for improvements on James Curries block Valued £399'. John planted lettuces and celery in the garden, put in more potatoes, ploughed and sowed barley. The ewes were lambing, but some lambs died in the cold. Catherine helped to plant melons, cucumbers and tomatoes, and John set and watched fires in some of the bigger trees. When he had a sore arm he worked in the house fixing a mantel, and then did some gardening and fencing. In October Syme came to help him build a fence, and John borrowed a lightning saw to cut big logs, and then made wooden blocks for the floor of the house. On 6 October a letter arrived from Neil to tell them that Jane had had a daughter. In the middle of October, Walter McKay set out for Bacchus Marsh and Ballan to collect and bring back his own and the Curries' cows. John paid him £3, and looked after his selection while he was away.

John borrowed George Grant's plough and harrow to prepare a paddock for maize and sorghum. McKay arrived back with the herd and John built a yard for the calves. From now on there would be twice-daily milking, seldom mentioned in Catherine's diary. John planted potatoes, and the children were sent out to look after the sheep, which kept wandering away to Grant's place. A great deal of time and energy was spent retrieving the livestock that wandered across the unfenced land. The building of the new house proceeded well, and by 10 November John was laying the floor. The next day Catherine recorded:

> *A young chap came and wanted to take a drawing of the place. I told him we would be glad to forget what it is like now as soon as possible.*

The painter, Charles Round, drew the McPherson's place instead. A muted but recurring theme in Catherine's diary is the wish to be surrounded by nice things, to have a pretty house, to have 'more singing' in her life.

In November the maize and sorghum was sown, carrots were planted in the garden and Catherine put pumpkins between the potatoes. John cut saplings to make temporary yards for cows and sheep, and to make a bail for milking. Seven-year-old Tom went out to help his father with the ringbarking and cutting of saplings. Cutting large trees was a risky business, and on 24 November John had to help Syme, who had nearly felled a tree on to his hut. At the end of November John was shearing, and cutting logs.

December was hot, and John was felling large trees at the bottom of the new garden. One was so large that it took six others with it as it fell, and a borrowed cart was smashed. John took good care of his horses, and used Dimple sparingly to pull the larger logs needed for fence posts. By 14 December John was not well, so he turned to the easier task of digging a water-hole for the cows. In the heat Catherine was making raspberry jam, baking bread, and occasionally doing milking for sick neighbours as well as coping with her own herd. John went back to cutting tea-tree in the swamp, and in his spare time made a trough for the horses. He took Tom with him when he went to help a neighbour with his ringbarking.

By the end of the year the initial euphoria of the new beginning was starting to fade. Maybe it could be put down to exhaustion. On 20 December Sandy McPherson came to collect money for the picnic on New Year's Day. Catherine gave him half a crown for each of the children but nothing for herself, 'as I was not pleased. I think they have treated me very shabby.' She and Bertie did not go to the picnic, but on New Year's Day 1877 she noted that others 'did not think much of the picnic'.

1877

There would never again be a January as happy as the first. January and February were the summer months for burning off, and people lit fires on hot, north-wind days. At the end of each year the selectors finished scrub cutting and prepared for the 'burn'. Once the tall timber had been felled, the thick scrub and the stumps had to be burned away. After the wet Gippsland winter and spring the undergrowth took some time to dry out, and several weeks of hot weather were needed to ensure a good burn. Many selectors waited for a hot north wind to fan the flames. Usually neighbours advised each other of an impending burn, and had several people to help light and watch the fires. No matter what precautions were taken, in the thick scrub the fires easily raged out of control, burning fences, huts and stock.

Everyone was uneasy and irritable at burning time, especially Catherine, who grew more and more afraid of the fire, and disturbed by the thick pall of smoke that hung over the farm. On 4 January there was the first rift with the Hardies. 'John told Hardie he was *Blethering* he was speaking about the fire and his *Impressions* of it.' Three days later Jos Hardie read the lesson at church but did not go home past the Curries; the 'Blethering', thought Catherine, 'had fairly disgusted him'. The next Sunday Catherine noted that 'Mrs. Jos Hardie went by and a lot of other strangers'. Shortly afterwards the children 'started to the new school' with the Hardie children, and the Hardie and Currie families began to visit again. On 21 January John held the first church service in the new school building. The permanent school had been built in 1877 by James Treeby for £69 6s 6d, and there was an average attendance of twenty-three, with thirty-five children on the roll.[25]

But Catherine was obviously not the easiest person to get along with. Her sense of her own dignity was strong, but made her vulnerable to slight, even imagined slight. She hated the 'impudence' of others, especially if she felt it was directed at John. She went to the Grants by invitation to arrange a dance at the school, but recorded on her return, 'I have nothing to do with it. I would not have as I could not see the object of it'. In February the schoolteacher sent a note to John asking for help in moving a log: 'such impudence', thought Catherine. Later in the month she went to visit Mrs Greenshields at her new farm which was 'not very far—wish it was farther'.

In February 1877 Neil and Jane arrived to stay, bringing their new baby, Ned. Ned had been born on 28 September, exactly nine months after the wedding, and was 'a nice little baby, and so good'. It was not long before there was another baby in the small house, for in March their neighbour Mrs Emms died, leaving a baby boy. Catherine brought him home, referring to him as if he were a little living parcel: 'I don't know how long I shall have to keep it but I could not leave it there'. Catherine cared for the little boy carefully, but he became sick on 24 March. Catherine sent for Mr Emms and later for a doctor, who did not arrive. The baby died on 29 March, and on 30 March sad

Mr Emms arrived with a coffin and a bottle of whisky. The next day John took the tiny coffin on his horse to the cemetery. In April Mr Emms brought Catherine a pig as a token of his thanks. The pig did not last very long either, and was dead by the end of the month. The diary is full of entries on the death of people and of stock, and sometimes it is hard to distinguish between the people and the cows and horses, since the Curries gave their livestock the names of their friends and relations. When Catherine records that she killed Sandy Lander, it takes a moment to realise that she means the pig and not the man.

The Symes bought the Lardner store from the Shaws, and in March John helped them to move in. Catherine's brother, Ned Wells, arrived to help with the 'piling'. One day Catherine got lost taking Ned his lunch, so the next day she and Ned 'made a track to his work without crossing a swamp'. John went to Melbourne again for more cocksfoot grass and clover. The back-breaking work of clearing went on, and John stripped tree-ferns to make a bigger space for the garden, and he and Catherine planted apple trees, currants, gooseberries and strawberries, carving out their tiny civilised plot in the middle of the wilderness. John began to build back rooms and a verandah on to the house, while Ned carted and chopped saplings, and then began to dig the potatoes. In May the men were clearing while the children gathered sticks, and Catherine made pumpkin jam and found a new place for her clothesline.

In June John was ploughing and raking, and planting plum and apple trees, and more currants and gooseberries in the garden while Catherine and James moved the strawberries. Ned went home on 10 June, and Catherine noted,

> *John settled with Ned. He asked and got £1 per week for all the time he has been here. I thought it far too much, as he has not worked half time, and given me twice more work than I would have had with a stranger.*

John went back to ploughing the potato paddock, Katie walking behind the plough to pick up any potatoes. John cleared and ploughed the barley and the hops paddock. On 14 July Catherine complained, 'I don't feel very well think I hurt myself when I was lost yesterday'. Locals lost their way coming home from visiting next-door neighbours, while strangers staggered out of the bush and had to be fed and given a bed for the night, before being pointed in the right direction in the morning. Livestock too often went missing for days, turning up in unusual places and causing trouble and conflict. The Murdie cattle now seemed to be under control, but in November Catherine noted that 'We had Jos Hardie cattle in the yard today and he had to come for them. He was Black and Impudent'.

A great many people were being impudent to Catherine. Margaret and John Syme were running the store, and Catherine recorded:

29.8   *I went to Mrs. Symes to see if she had any boots that would fit me had not any. I think she was in a very Bad Temper as I expected to get the money for the Sunday school but thought she gave me abuse instead.*

John was also having trouble with unreasonable people. The meetings about the new shire were very rough, and he was not properly appreciated on the church committee. He resigned in June, and refused to read any more in November. Catherine was upset, but John advised her not to worry too much about the insults of other people, as it was nearly always due to ignorance.

Meanwhile John continued the clearing, Catherine went to borrow a sieve to sift the oats, and planted radish seed, cabbages and lettuces. John grafted a ripston pippin apple tree, a cherry and a pear tree. Now the farm was beginning to produce some saleable produce. By August the oats had been gathered, and the Curries began selling them to neighbours. John built a dairy and Catherine made butter, although she had constant trouble finding a buyer. In Ballan this had been no problem, as the big Ballarat market was close. But Melbourne was the large market for Gippsland dairy farmers, and by the time the butter reached the capital over roads that became quagmires after rain, much of it was fit only to grease axles or be turned into confectionery.

Catherine tried several local buyers. On 5 December she sent twelve pounds of butter to Mr Rintels (called Brintels, or sometimes Brintnalls, in the diary), and four days later dispatched another fourteen pounds. The next day she recorded, 'Went to Brintels to get settled for the butter. He says I must not send any more yet as he don't know what to do with it'. This would be a recurring problem for Catherine. In December she recorded, 'First cheese I have made in Gippsland', and she was beginning to make strawberry jam from the fruit of their strawberry bed. The children helped with the lighter work, such as picking up sticks. Sunday was partially a rest day, but there was still the twice-daily milking to be done.

1878

Catherine refused to go to the 1878 New Year dinner dance, and January was a nervous month. Fires were burning all around the Currie farm, fences were burned down and frightened animals roamed the district. Sandy Grant died on 18 January at the age of forty-six. His obituary helped to explain why Catherine had found him so easy to put up with:

> Mr Grant hailed from the Highlands of Scotland, and possessed many of the characteristics of the Celtic race. He was open and generous in his disposition, with a warm heart and open hand, sincere and steadfast in his friendship, and is said to leave not one enemy behind him.[26]

In March, a serious and long lasting worry began for the family. Tom came home from school with a pain in the knee, feeling sick. John thought that he had been in the sun without his hat, and had growing pains in his knee. Mr Hardie came with his doctor's book and gave him a dose for bile, and Catherine treated the knee with kerosene oil. In April Mrs Syme advised poulticing and Maggie McPherson brought linseed meal. Catherine distrusted doctors, and it was not until 22 April that the leg broke and ran with 'bad like stuff'. In May Mr Aspinall came, to no great welcome from Catherine—'and a perfect Adonis he thinks himself'. The leg continued to worsen until June, when a large piece of bone came out of it. Other small pieces floated to the surface, and by 23 June nine pieces of bone had come out of his leg. It was not until the end of the month that Tom was finally able to get about without a stick.

A modern opinion suggests that Tom had osteomyelitis. Even a farming family, used to dealing with sick and wounded animals, would not have been able to make this diagnosis. The failure was certainly not one of neglect. Catherine worried constantly about her children, and Tom's leg, which would bother him for the rest of his life, was a continuing source of worry to her. Tom seemed to be the favoured child, at least the favoured son, and perhaps the failure to deal with his injured leg added to her concern for him.

Late in September there was another trauma when John was called to look after old Walter McKay, who had been attacked by Syme and nearly killed. Catherine recorded:

26.9 *Old Mac he was such a quiet old fellow. John has taken him to Drouin today. He lent the poor old man £2 10s and paid other expences for him. I am afraid it will all be lost as John thinks he will not get better. I was very glad to see John home tonight as I was afraid he might have had to go to Melbourne with Mac.*

27.9 *Syme here this morning says he wants a bag of chaff. I wonder if it is to make his bed when he is hiding from the police. The policeman here looking for Syme. I hear he has taken him up . . .*

28.9 *Heard we had seen the last of poor old McKay. He died yesterday morning. I wonder how it will be for Syme now and if we will get the money he owed us.*

Syme appeared to have escaped retribution, and apparently few grudges were held by the Curries, for he was soon back in the district and visiting again. On 13 November John put in a claim for £14 on McKay's estate.

1879

The end of the year saw dances and children's parties, for the hard-working community made sure there was plenty of entertainment. But Catherine was still complaining about neighbours, and was suffering terrible toothache. The New Year of 1879 began again with fires, and James Currie's hut was burned down. At the beginning of February, Catherine recorded:

5.2 *. . . Mrs. Hardie sent to tell us that their fire had come to us at the Whiskey Ck road. I went to see, knocked down some fence, it is all Burned from the swamp to the hill. Mrs. Syme came, with a Bottle and grog for the men, she had too much herself and scolded terribly. We are watching fires both sides now.*

Catherine could not sit at home, but went out to the fires, raking to help make fire breaks, and returning home to record in her diary her prayers for rain.

By the end of February the fires were abating, and the children came home from school with the good news that both Katie and Tom had passed their certificates. From this time the children would only go to school when they were not needed to work on the farm. There were some pleasures and outings. May 20 was a good day for Catherine, and she recorded:

> *Mrs. Greenshields gave me my petticoat that she had been flowering for me, it is very pretty. I met John at McPhersons had tea there and some music and got home about 10 o'clock.*

In May John started to build a new hut for James, although all did not appear well with James and in September he became lost while trying to go to one of the paddocks. James was now almost blind, and was becoming confused. On 17 September Catherine's first neighbour, Mrs Jos Hardie, came to say goodbye, for the Hardies were leaving to live in town. They did not sell their property, and would reappear in the district and the diary at a later date. The new life begun so hopefully had turned out to be hard and unrewarding. In October Catherine noted:

3.10   *The old sow eat all the young goose eggs yesterday. I am so sorry and cross I don't know what to do, everything seems to go contrary, a hen killed one of the little chickens the cows were far away this morning they are all away to the paddock to clear. It seem all work and no good coming of it.*

Part of Catherine's despair and exhaustion was explained in November. On 15 November John took up the diary:

> *The Climax. Kate had a daughter this morning about 3 o'clock, a fine child fat and big. Planting spuds and harrowing, came home early.*

Catherine's sister Lizzie had come to help with the new baby, who was officially named Isabell Jean, but was known to the family as Ann. By December Catherine was back to her routine of butter-making, and had paid her subscription to the New Year picnic.

The years did not vary greatly. Once the house had been finished, a dairy and a barn were still to be built. In May 1878 George Grant had come to tell the Curries of a new cheese factory planned by Charles Harkness and George Murdie. John Currie took some part in its establishment, and it eventually became a thriving concern under the management of Mr Shiels.[27] Oats and hay were reaped in the summer heat, potatoes were dug and planted, and lambs killed for meat. The ploughing and fencing, harrowing and gardening went on constantly. The dairy herd grew, and Catherine milked and made butter and cheese. Through it all ran the terse entry, 'clearing'.

To transform this landscape, the first optimistic settlers thought, all that was needed was hard work. For Catherine, hard work was a simple fact of life. The work she recorded in the diary was mainly that performed outside the house: clearing the land, planting a garden, fencing, milking and butter-making. She rarely spoke of the daily grind of keeping the house in order and the family decently fed and clothed. We are left to imagine the tasks of keeping the small slab hut clean, of scrubbing boots caked in mud, or clothes ingrained with soil after a hard day's clearing or planting. Clothes and nappies had to be carried to the stream and washed by hand, while water was carried from the same place until a well had been dug. Through the long wet winters the elaborate clothing of the day would be dried in front of the fire, and through the hot dry summers the bread would be baked and meals cooked on the wood stove in the small and steamy kitchen. Freshly killed meat had to be cooked or cured immediately, as there was no refrigeration and the ice-man did not call. Sides of bacon were hung to cure in the kitchen, and Catherine made sausages and black puddings. She did not record many of her labours in the house, apart from the less common tasks such as seasonal jam-making. It was outside in the bush that the real work took place. For John Currie also, hard work was a simple fact of life.

In their first three years, the Curries were required to cultivate at least 10 per cent of their land. In a letter to the Board of Land John reported the results of his work. By 1878 he had twenty-two acres under grass, seven acres of potatoes and three and a half acres of oats. His four-roomed wooden dwelling measured twenty-eight by twenty-two feet, and his barn of paling and shingles was forty by thirty-four feet. In the first year after planting, his two-and-a-half acre potato field had yielded a ton, in the second year he gathered four tons from seven acres. John had also done a great deal of the work of clearing and planting on James's larger property, Hartwood, where by 1878 there were sixteen acres under oats and potatoes, a slab and bark house measuring ten by twelve feet, and a hut of ten by eight feet. John noted that he could not complete the required fencing on his property, owing to the density of the scrub.[28]

Some of John's neighbours had cleared more land than he had, and had fulfilled all the licence requirements, often with the help of hired labour. John, however, with two properties to work and with James failing in health and eyesight, was trying to do nearly all the work himself. Like digging for gold, the search for wealth from the land involved some hard and dirty work, and only the best equipped and organised, and perhaps the luckiest, would serenely survive the rigours of the new life.

Landscape

No landscape is permanent, and every new landscape is dangerous until it has been rendered familiar by time and use, dream and myth. The land created *ab origine*, from the beginning, belonged to the dreamers who had created it. Geographical orientation, says Eliade, is related to mythical history: 'The mythical history that transformed a "chaotic land" into a sacred and articulated world helps, moreover, to bind together groups and tribes'.[29] By 1788 at least 1600 generations of people had been born and died in Australia.[30] There had been time to create a land of sky gods and to tell stories of all those ancestors who had joined the gods. This was a land of people who had lived and died in the same landscape, who had dreamed the land and re-created it many times in ritual and myth.

The western section of the East Gippsland forest, which would become home to the Currie family, was full of animals, birds and plant life which had supported the Aboriginal tribes of the Kulin and the Kurnai for thousands of years. The bush provided food for its inhabitants: daisy yam roots were dug up and roasted, bracken roots were ground into a paste and roasted in hot ashes to make bread. Lyrebirds, koalas, possums and wallabies were hunted for meat and skins, and bark was used to make shelters. The people took care of their forest and food supply, and regularly made use of fire to clear out the thick undergrowth and encourage new growth.[31]

Natural selection had ensured the survival of the forest and the animals and people who depended upon it. This fine balance was precarious, and would soon be disrupted as gold seekers and settlers followed close behind the first white explorers. The Kulin and Kurnai people who had fished and hunted in this isolated corner of the world were soon to be supplanted, and their life-style destroyed along with the bush. As no Aboriginal words had been written to describe this process, our understanding of this cataclysmic change comes from white words. The modern poet and historian Laurie Duggan has expressed his version and understanding of their fate:

> And a message
> passed from tribe to tribe
> that the sky's props were rotten
> and unless men were sent
> to cut new poles
> the sky would cave in and kill everybody . . .[32]

The sky did soon cave in on the hunters and gatherers, and while it did not quite kill everybody, it did kill off an old way of life and the means of survival for those who had considered the forest their own. The deliberate and articulate white man had a different version of events to leave for posterity and this story did not say that the sky had caved in, but that it had been opened up to shed light upon the new world:

> Large portions of Australia which a few years ago were covered with dense forests and inhabited only by a savage race presents now a very different aspect. The night of ignorance and barbarism is chased from those regions by the cheering influences of civilization.[33]

The area of eastern Victoria now known as Gippsland extends south and east of Melbourne, down and out towards the coast. The first white explorers were Scottish pastoralists who came down from the north in search of land, and travellers who came in from the sea at Port Albert on the south coast. As early as 1841 a party from the *Singapore* left Port Albert to find a stock route to Melbourne. One of the party, W. A. Brodribb, described the journey through the forests that would become familiar to pioneering selectors some thirty years later:

> The thick high scrub was bound together by strong vines, which so impeded our progress that we had at last to take it in turns to cut away the obstruction with our tomahawks. Sometimes we came upon the huge trunk of a fallen tree which completely barred our path, so that we had, in a similar manner, to cut a path around the monster . . . Scarcely a day passed that we were not drenched with rain.[34]

Travelling at the rate of about half a mile a day, the party eventually reached Melbourne via Western Port. Other travellers also found the going difficult. In 1843 the surveyor of the newly proclaimed squatting district of Western Port, Charles Tyers, set out overland from Melbourne to Port Albert, but the swampy country was flooded by recent rains, and he was forced to return to Melbourne and board a ship for Port Albert.

The Europeans began to appropriate the land by naming the flora and fauna. Despite its European common name, the mountain ash of Australia is a eucalypt (*Eucalyptus regnans*), and regularly grows to a height of ninety metres if spared by fire and axes. The fallen trunk of a mountain ash was measured by a surveyor in the 1880s at over 130 metres, the tallest tree ever recorded. Not even the Californian redwood, generally considered to be the tallest tree in the world, has produced a specimen to better this record. In a forest, the roots of the mountain ash trees mingle and lock together, and the high leaf canopy allows through just enough light to enable vines and ferns to flourish on the ground in a thick tangle beneath the trees. Given this thick matting on the forest floor, no new seeds can find a place to grow, and the mountain ash can only propagate after a fire. The trees are highly inflammable, and once a bushfire starts, a fire ball will rip through the canopy, releasing seeds from their pods to fall to the now cleared forest floor. The seeds germinate and the strongest saplings spring up at an amazing rate, renewing the forest within a few years.

The ancient forests of Gippsland were made up of the giant mountain ash and other species of eucalypt, including messmate (*Eucalyptus obliqua*), blackbutt (*Eucalyptus pilularis*) and blue gum (*Eucalyptus globulus*). Under good conditions these could all attain heights of more than sixty metres. Blue and white gums could grow to a height of forty-five to sixty metres, with a diameter of one to two metres, while the blackbutts could reach ninety metres in height with diameters of two and a half to three metres. Between the giant trees were pockets of tall and densely packed timber which the early settlers called hazel scrub and which grew to fifteen or twenty metres. On the soggy forest floor grew tree-ferns, musk and wire grass.[35]

The Selection Acts of the 1860s determined that the country would be opened up for settlement, and with free selection in 1870, the requirement to clear 10 per cent of the land within three years made the destruction of the forest by fire and ringbarking even more rapid. The tracks travelled by the intending selectors were first established by government surveyors such as John Lardner, and these were people trained to deal in straight lines. This seemed to the European mind the most economic and rational way to divide land into neat parcels for the selectors, usually without reference to the local topography. In the Gippsland forest, the great problem for the first selectors would be to build fences along the imaginary lines drawn so neatly upon the surveyor's map.

It was not so easy for the surveyor to achieve the straight line, either. When Lardner drove his track from the Old Sale Road at Brandy Creek, he had to cut through a dense jungle, a tangle of vines and ferns and bushes growing beneath the immense eucalypts. Even when coach tracks had been cut through the forests, the height and density of the forest amazed the traveller. David Brown, an early arrival, described his first impressions. 'What we saw was like living in a new world. On each side of the coach track a wall of undergrowth from fifty to sixty feet high. We could feel no wind, although you could hear it above the tree tops.' Brown described the forest cover by dividing it into two types: hazel and messmate. The messmate country was more open, but the hazel country was preferred by the settlers who thought it indicated richer soil. Brown described the hazels:

> ... the Hazels long spars from 1, 2, 3, 4 to 6 inches in diameter reaching up to thirty and forty feet in height interspersed with Gum Saplings like Telegraph Poles reaching up to sixty and seventy feet in height, mixed with these would [be] tall fern trees and musks in this dense mass of vegetation, to penetrate it you would have to go in places edge on and if you wanted to go in any distance, unless you blaised your track you would have a difficulty in finding your way out.[36]

It was into this wilderness that the selectors dragged wives and children, pots and pans, livestock and startling optimism. The land which grew trees and scrub in such abundance would support their crops and pastures, the native birds and animals would be forced to give way to dairy cattle, sheep and horses. All that was needed for this transformation was hard work.

If you go now to the place where the Curries built their first small hut among the mountain ash trees more than a hundred years ago, you will not recognise it as the same place described in the diary. This is a landscape that has been deconstructed and reassembled to form another view. Travelling swiftly from Melbourne in a comfortable car, the modern traveller will reach the place where Lardner's Track turns off from the main highway. This is a land of green and gentle hills, with occasional stands of old gum trees to reduce the monotony, with paddocks of rich brown earth furrowed by tractors, with houses dotted within friendly sight of one another. The house Catherine Currie occupied in the last years of her life stands in this new landscape. It is a weatherboard house with a wide verandah; it has a fine garden and a well-built barn filled with ancient machinery. But this is not the house that John built for his family when he first arrived at his new selection.

The Curries settled on a hill. They had already built themselves one house on a hill, and they obviously liked an elevated position. While many selectors built close to a water supply, John and Catherine chose a site that would eventually give them magnificent views across their own land, even though they had to pay for such foresight by digging a very deep well, and by dragging all their supplies up the steep track to their hut. They dug their deep well and cleared a tiny garden, where Catherine planted a chestnut tree. This first hut is long gone, burnt in a bushfire. The only way now to identify the site of the first house is by the stump of the old chestnut tree, recently cut down, and a deep well covered over with wire netting.

Today the site is in the middle of a paddock, in season planted with potatoes by the manager of the Warragul Field Days organisation to whom the land belongs. If you go to the top of the hill just after ploughing, you may find the remains of a destroyed domesticity: old pieces of china, smashed and crazy, mostly blue and white, and pieces of glass, fused by the fierce heat of a bushfire. In the distance, across the cleared paddocks, there is a fine view of the chimneys of the Drouin butter factory.

It is hard, standing on the hilltop in the middle of this serene landscape, smashed willow-pattern crockery in hand, to imagine the first landscape as seen by the Curries in 1875. Then the Drouin butter factory was a distant dream, their hill was shrouded in trees, the houses of the few neighbours were hidden in the forest, and the valleys they had to cross to visit their neighbours were swampy bogs. The present, re-formed landscape is the production of the Curries and their fellow selectors. It is the tangible production of a myth.

When John had cut down some of the biggest trees on his land, he turned to scrub and fern cutting. In the gullies and swamps the tree-ferns could grow to six or twelve metres. Among the scrub grew sword-grass and wire-grass, both with cutting edges that could severely damage the scrub-cutter's hands. Once a clearing had been cut in the scrub, the vertical sections rising on each side would reveal layers of scrub and trees, sometimes rising sixty metres above the ground. An early pioneer left a description of these layers: the bottom strata showed fallen logs and saplings covered by sword-grass, the next was composed of bare stems with a thick canopy of scrub, out of which rose the towering trunks of trees. Thick foliage at the highest strata made sure that very little sunlight filtered through to the perpetually sodden earth.[37]

In later years John and Catherine's daughter Fern wrote a letter to the Lands Department complaining that her father had missed out on 'the easily managed hazel country':

My father did not get the block of land which he pegged, in company with his neighbours from Ballan. When he returned in a month or two to find it claimed, he took the nearest alternative available, which unfortunately was on the wrong side of the swamp. Instead of the easily managed hazel country, when timber was 'rung', up came willow, dogwood . . . a constant watch had to be kept, in after years, on the original scrub.[38]

The hazel scrub grew among the blue gums and blackbutt, and consisted of hazels, some blackwoods and wattles, with ferns, wire-grass and sword-grass at the base. The timber was easier to cut and the hazel scrub burned easily, but it often grew on lighter soil. The land John Currie selected was more difficult to clear, and the scrub more difficult to burn, and after a poor burn the scrub flourished once more.[39] But the soil he was gradually uncovering was rich and fertile.

Catherine was interested in the natural world. She often recorded in her diary the appearance of comets, or noted an eclipse of the sun. The trees, however, stood between her and the domesticated, benign farming landscape that would be the eventual outcome of all the family's efforts. The trees did not yield easily, and they had to be burned as well as felled if the rules of selection were to be kept. The giant eucalypts harboured and spread the fires that terrified Catherine. They sometimes inflicted injuries upon her husband and son as they struggled to fell and burn them, and they even killed neighbours and stock. They fell in high winds, randomly and without warning. Ringbarked skeletons, the standing casualties of clearing, could crumble suddenly, smashing houses or carts and jeopardising all that had been achieved. On 5 December, the diary noted,

John felling trees at the bottom of where the garden is to be fell one last night and it lodged and he cut another to let it down and then six went altogether . . . the big tree John was felling went clean the opposite way it should have came right in the yard broke Mack's cart a little.

The bush was full of life, some of it interesting, some of it dangerous and destructive. In the bush were koalas and lyrebirds, and Catherine noted her first sighting of the 'great hawk' with some awe, but her admiration was modified some time later when a white hawk took one of the chickens. John set a trap for it, and it was caught, uninjured. Catherine put it in a box, but there is no further reference to it. One night in July she noted that there was 'dreadful corroboree' among the wild dogs, and several days later the dingos took one of Hardie's sheep. The farmers began to poison the dogs, but Catherine discriminated between the dangerous and the beautiful, and was less pleased when people killed any of the harmless animals. The Syme's son David killed some little birds with his shotgun in September, and Catherine noted, 'poor little things they are so quiet it is such a pity'.

Catherine noted the 'iguanas' and 'porcupines' they saw, and in August 'walked up James survey line got a bunch of blossom and heath so pretty'. But the bush also harboured the 'bears' that frightened the children, and the wallabies that ate the precious grass.* There were plagues of caterpillars that threatened their livelihood, and the ferns were home to snakes. The natural world could be beautiful, but every landscape is dangerous, especially before it is tamed. While John struggled to create his paddocks, Catherine worked on a more manageable space: the garden that would separate her from the forest.

Speaking of his book *The Road to Botany Bay*, Paul Carter remarks on the creation of space by naming:

---

* The iguana of the diary could refer to the one species of goanna found in Gippsland, but is more likely to be a large lizard. The frequently mentioned 'bears' are most likely to be wombats.

A woman, say, in Gippsland, describing in her memoirs the act of settlement, does so in terms of the creation of small but eloquent boundaries, symbolic places where speech and memories can congregate. She progressively covers a chair, puts a curtain across a window, gets the fence up at the bottom of the paddock. These events, recorded in her diary, actually evoke her history directly in terms of spatial enclosures—and their transgression.

For those boundaries don't exist to shut out the bush; the bush becomes an attractive ferny dell at the very moment it is on the other side of the boundary. Definably different from the stump of the mountain ash symbolically preserved inside the garden and domesticated with geraniums, the wilderness now becomes an object which can be described and loved . . . it can be photographed, you can go for walks there—walks which are no longer exploratory, but are now acts of exploratory reminiscence.[40]

The boundary, Carter suggests, is a place where communication takes place, where a dialogue occurs. This is a communication between the known and the unknown, the enclosed and the unenclosed. The boundary is a place where some kind of interaction takes place; it consists of meeting grounds, 'neutral places where exchanges could occur'.

The garden, into which Catherine and John put so much time and energy, was a symbol of the new world they were working towards. It fed the family with familiar foods and it grew familiar flowers to please the eye. It was proof that human will could triumph over natural forces and that millions of years of evolution could be changed by something other than chance. Eventually, the Curries hoped, the whole property would become a garden, but meanwhile their small and bounded plot was an oasis in the wilderness. It would even achieve limited fame. The reporter of the *South Gippsland Express*, 'The Bohemian', came across the well-established Currie garden on 24 January 1884:

We piloted our way through and over fences, down gullies and up hills until we arrived at Mr Currie's, and it beginning to get dark we decided to go no farther. We therefore dismounted, and were introduced to the fruit garden by Mrs Currie, while we awaited the return of the 'gude man' himself. And I must give the palm to this as being the very best of the farmer's gardens which I had come across during the whole of my journey through the district. It is well kept, and being splendid soil grows all kinds of fruit. Strawberries and raspberries were here in abundance—at least when we went there, but I fancy the crop suffered considerably ere we left.

There were many who could see beauty in this wild land, but they appreciated it most after it had been brought into manageable proportions. Once the hard work had been finished, there could be nostalgia for the wilderness that had gone. The poet Nellie Clerk was the wife of a selector near Korumburra and unusually sensitive to the competing claims of preservation and progress. In 'To My First Garden Flower' she imagined the feelings of these giants of the forest as they were felled, but significantly such thoughts arose from a contemplation of the first blooming of an imported species:

> Short a monarch's life was clipt
> Where you reign, Geranium!
> There once a mighty Eucalypt
> High plumes in heaven's azure dipped,
> And cumbrous bark robes yearly stripped,
> Revealing hidden beauty.
>
> Great the fall that left a throne
> For you, royal Geranium!
> The cruel axe cleft though the bone

Landscape

With rattling crash and thunderous groan,
He fell! a cairn of soft sandstone
I built to mourn his beauty.

In another poem, 'My Gippsland Home', she welcomed with mixed feelings the clearing of the forest for gardens:

And my garden extends where the ridge southward bends
By picket fence jealously guarded,
And flowers and fruits and edible roots,
Each season's light toils have rewarded.

Far to west and to north, great clearings stretch forth,
Herds and flocks and fat pastures revealing,
'Twixt dead trees that stand grey and gaunt o'er the land,
With bare arms to heaven appealing.

There, axes and fires have wrought my desire,
Before them the matted scrub sweeping;
But armies of these ghostly eucalypt trees
For years their sad guard will be keeping.[41]

It seems that there was more nostalgia for the giant trees than for the Aboriginal people who were now usurped as keepers of the landscape. The men who had been sent to cut the new poles to prop up the sky had changed the perspective and the view of the sky and the land. The landscape had been irretrievably remade in the image of the latest settlers, who had changed its colour and its form. But there was a cost, a price still to be calculated.

All the hard work, and all the words spoken and written, could not mask the absence at the heart of things, the fact of living in a landscape which had not yet been appropriated into dream and myth and which was, indeed, the enemy. David Malouf, in his novel *Remembering Babylon*, speaks of another settler's wife, a fictional wife who lives in Queensland. For her it was the palpable absence of her own history which was the problem with the new land:

> It was the fearful loneliness of the place that most affected her—the absence of ghosts.
>
> Till they arrived no other lives had been lived here. It made the air that much thinner, harder to breathe. She had not understood, till she came to a place where it was lacking, the extent to which her sense of the world had to do with the presence of those who had been there before, leaving signs of their passing and spaces still warm with breath—a threshold worn with the coming and going of feet, hedges between fields that went back a thousand years, and the names even further; most of all, the names on headstones, which were *their* names, under which lay the bones that had made their bones and given them breath.
>
> They would be the first dead here. It made death that much lonelier, and life lonelier too.[42]

Eventually, the reconstructed landscape would be filled with a new history, with the breath of a known people, and with the names on headstones which told of life and death. But this would be a different landscape. For now, as the trees that had meant life to previous generations burned and crashed to the forest floor, the boundary between the past and the future was made explicit in the blackened and ring-barked landscape. The props that had held up the sky were under attack, and the men sent to cut the new poles had not yet triumphed. In this landscape, life would have to be uneasy.

Blighted Hopes 1880–1882

1880

The years now always began badly. On New Year's Day of 1880 Catherine went to the picnic but did not enjoy it. The family provided an occasional smile, and when Grandaa arrived to visit from the Cunningham's on 15 January, he was 'wearing Mrs Wells's Sunday Hat, said he could not carry it any other way without being crushed'. There is occasional reference to Grandaa and 'Mrs Wells', who may be the wife of Leaper Wells junior, unless Grandaa has married again. It was very hot for the reaping, and the Curries were being bothered by 'strange cattle' that were invading their property, and had to be driven away from the precious water supply.

On 26 January Catherine went to Drouin to 'take the cheque for the rest of James Curries block', but on 30 January she recorded, 'James new Hut was burned down sometime yesterday and everything in it, just yesterday twelve months it was burned with the Bush fires.' The Curries were very busy selling their potatoes, and earning about £1 for five hundredweight, but despite the hard work, Catherine still found time to worry, and by February she was in a fine state of nerves. People began burning off, and she carefully noted the direction of the wind every morning, and prayed for rain. It was not long before her worst fears were realised.

12.1 *. . . the fence caught fire a piece of it Burned and the wind got very high. Oh I am so frightened, fairly miserable—we will have to try and get away from here after this. Oh how I wish it would rain before morning. Daa and Katie is out looking how the trees are burning now half past nine PM. Neil was here this morning, came for the Bridle and brought home the baby's swing—we did not want it and tried to make him take it back but he is so proud he would not, it is part of the log fence around the potatoes that is Burnt the wind is very high indeed since four or five o'clock this evening.*

. . .

19.2 *[John] says he will see if Mr. Bailly can get a buyer for the Place as we can never live here to be burned out some day oh I can't stand it at all I am so frightened I can do nothing but watch the smoke and wish for rain.*

It seems that John was not as worried about fire as Catherine, for the next day he set off with Katie and Tom to visit the Jubilee Exhibition in Melbourne. Catherine stayed up all night to get them ready for the trip. Maybe John had only suggested selling to calm Catherine's nerves, for no more was said of it, and life settled back into routine once the fires had passed. In February the rains came, and it was too wet to visit little John Currie Cunningham for his birthday on 28 February. But Catherine's nerves were still badly frayed, and she worried that John would light a fire to burn the stubble. When John failed to return home when expected one evening in March, she became panic-stricken, imagining him lying dead or injured in the bush. It was all a misunderstanding, but Catherine noted, 'I was certainly never in the same difficulty before'. Small events were beginning to take on the shape of large tragedies.

On 16 March Catherine sold some of her butter to Mr Sinclair, who had opened Stout's store in Drouin. He paid her a shilling per pound for eighteen pounds. John was cutting shingles for a new stable and working at McEvoys. It seems that John and McEvoy were working together, and maybe share farming. The council was working on a road down in the swamp, and on 1 March John attended a council meeting to see what was happening. Catherine sold some eggs from the chickens and the geese, but could not sell any more butter. On 26 March her brother Lep arrived from Melbourne, and it must have been some time since she had seen him, for she remarked, 'I should not have known him'. Jane came to visit the next day. On 30 March a policeman arrived, on his way to fine McEvoy for not sending his children to school.

As his hut had burned down, James may have been living with his brother's family, and he was certainly working on the farm, for Catherine noted on 1 April that he was grubbing stumps with Tom. On 15 April he went off by himself and could not be found for some time. Eventually he turned up again, but it was obvious that he could no longer live alone, and John started to build him a room next to the new stable. April was spent digging potatoes, and Catherine was still having trouble selling her butter. John made some new pigstys in May, and Catherine killed a snake in the fireplace. She made forty pounds of butter in 'oblong squares', hoping it would sell better that way in Melbourne. She injured her thumb, but dressed it in gin and spent a few days visiting neighbours and trying to collect unpaid debts for the sale of their produce. On 25 May she sent twenty-four pounds of butter to Mr Taylor in Melbourne.

In June John went to Drouin to attend an Indignation Meeting against the division of the shire into ridings. Catherine sent her butter in with him to the new store, but the owner would not take it and John eventually took it to Sinclair. Catherine went to clear the school track, and annoyed Neil Cunningham by trying to make him take home a rhubarb root he didn't want—'I pressed him all I could', she said. The diary implies that Neil is an unreasonable man, and much too hard on Jane. John finished building the stable, and Sinclair took another eight pounds of butter at 9d per pound. The Curries planted rhubarb, raspberries and strawberries. John was attending political meetings and went to Drouin to hear Mr Berry, the ex-premier. Butter fell to 8d per pound, and Catherine sold some pigs.

In July John started to plough, and a friend visited to tell of the Kelly capture. Catherine continued to sell her butter, and went to stay overnight at Woodene with Jane. On 9 July Tom took seven pounds of butter to Drouin, but 'they told him not to bring any more. Those Drouin shopkeepers all want drowning. I don't know what we shall do with our Produce', Catherine complained. One thing they had plenty of was ferns, and they sold some to Mr Boade for a shilling each. John was threshing oats and ploughing, with Katie and Tom picking up sticks before the plough. On 14 July John went to vote against Mr Service's Reform Bill.

On 26 July John went to see Mr Stewart to find out if he wanted any oats. Catherine noted, 'his man left a message with James on Friday, but we could not make head or tail of it'. James, it seems, was no longer responsible enough to convey sensible messages. Catherine was selling her butter to neighbours, and occasionally to Sinclair. In August her nightmare returned in a different form when the Kenlocks' house was burned down, not in a bushfire, but by accident. Catherine noted, 'they were near being burned in their beds. They just had it done up so nicely too'. There were men working on the road, and on 3 August 'John clearing a track to the gate at the south side near the swamp as the road men wants him to help them tomorrow'. On 12 August John went to Drouin to vote in the council elections and join the Loyal Liberal Union. Catherine bought a dog called Bob for ten shillings, and noted, 'Katie and I are going to do without sugar to our tea for 3 month to save the price of him'. On 14 August Lizzie arrived on her way to the Cunninghams, the first intimation in the diary that there was another baby on the way. When Jane had a new daughter, 13-year-old Katie went to milk her cows for her.

Catherine was busy delivering oats, chaff and potatoes to neighbouring buyers, and selling duck and hen eggs and butter. In September she recorded the sale of twenty bushels of oats at 2s 6d a bushel. On 11 October she noted, 'Bert went to school by himself today. Katie went to the swamp with him and Tom went and met him'. The older children did not have time to go to school—there was too much work to be done on the farm. John shot a wallaby in the corn, and Catherine made soup. John refused to taste it, but Jane, who was staying for a few days, thought it was 'capital'. In November a letter arrived from Catherine's sister Annie, to say that their sister Alice had died, leaving six young children. Tom started going back to school, and on 23 November John, Katie and Tom went to a dance at the school. This November entry is the last in the diary until 12 December.

The next entry begins again with an account of the work of the farm, cutting hops and planting potatoes. Then Catherine gets to the real story.

14.12   *. . . I had no heart to fill up my book since we lost our* wee pet *on the 24th of last month, it was oh so sudden. I was getting the Dinner Tea ready I carried her to the hole to dip a bucket of water. I stood her down and dipped it and she had a drink out the bucket, I led her by the hand to the door and said to her come in selfie Dearie and I feel sure she came in and went back to see where I got the water. I missed her a few minutes after, and ran to the back yard, looking and calling on her. I thought she must have followed Katie when she went for the cows then I asked Bertie if the front* *door was open. He said yes serta meaning half open. I then ran to the water hole. The first thing I saw was a little foam on the water. My heart told me what that was oh shall I ever forget it, I looked under the sticks and saw my wee pet, but oh dear I never thought it was too late, as she was such a short time in. I did the best I knew for her, and Mrs. and Mr. McPherson came but oh we lost her my heart is breaking and I feel frightened to grieve for fear I am punished even more severely, for it must have been as a punishment that she was taken from us like that. I can't help blaming myself for letting her out of my mind—where was she then but I thought she was playing at the back. For I loved her oh so much. We buried her at Drouin. Mr. Tracy made the coffin Mr. Sinclair lent his spring cart. Tom went, Jane was here with her Baby and a lot of the neighbours but I was nearly distracted and hardly know what I was doing, if I do yet. She seems never to be out of my mind though I know she is better than I can do for her, but she was so clever, there was never one so knowing of her age.*

The work went on. Sister Annie, who had arrived to help, went home, and the shearing began. The shears were blunt and old, and Catherine had to stand beside John and sharpen them all the time. Katie had to make the cheese, 'and it looks as though it was made of little stones', said Catherine in exasperation. Christmas Day was spent picking raspberries, and John, Katie and Tom went fishing.

1881

The year of 1881 began with everyone on edge. John sent his wool to 'Messrs Goldborough and Co', and Catherine bought some 'Black French Moire' for a dress. Grasshoppers were eating the turnips and carrots, and possums were destroying the oats. Poor little Bertie, only five years old, was having a hard time.

13.1   *I had to go to school with Bertie. I tried to make him go through Kenlocks paddock by himself. I whipped him and pelted him with sticks, but he would not go he is very frightened. He says it is for snakes and bears.*

     . . .

17.1   *Bertie not going to school today taking lessons at home.*

In February the fires began again, after John tried to burn a tree. The sparks were shooting everywhere, and when John tried to chop down the tree he discovered that his axe handle had been burnt. On 8 February James had 'some sort of Tantrum. Started swearing most dreadfully called me a B—and went off somewhere. Did not come to dinner when called. I can't think what has huffed him'. There was welcome rain and hail in March, but in April Catherine was remarking that Neil was an 'old humbug', and in May the news came that Joseph Hardie had been killed in a shipwreck off New Zealand. He had been working as chief engineer on the *Terana*. Mrs Hardie came back to live on the Hardie property, and called to visit Catherine in July.

12.7   *Mrs. Jos Hardie here. Poor Mrs. Jos it must be very hard for her to come here now. She says this place caused all their sorrows as her husband lost his life in looking for his health that he lost here.*

Catherine spent a great deal of her time calling on neighbours to collect payment for the produce the Curries had sold. There was a good deal of barter, as cash was a problem. On 9 June, Catherine noted,

Tom took 6 lbs salt butter to Mrs Simper did not get paid as he had not change for a note. He went to the Bank paid in the £10 note and brought home the bank book and some loose cheques as they had no cheque books.

On 13 June John took twenty-four bushels of oats to Mr Sinclair, but 'nothing said about money yet', and the next day Catherine was pleased to get a cheque for £1 3s 9d for some fowls she had sold. The season had not been a good one, and Catherine was trying to sell some sheep, as there was not enough feed for them. The Curries were selling oats and potatoes, and Mr Gregory bought twenty sheep skins from them for 1s 6d each. The Currie garden also provided an income.

28.6   *Mr and Mrs Bowman here he paid me for 8¼ bushells of oats and 3 Ducks at 2s each, 30s in all. He got some Bundel of Straw and some Plants out of the garden. Strawberries and Brocalie and cabbage plants and a white mulberry and a scented verbena and a lavender root.*

In the midst of all this activity, Catherine noted on 11 July, 'I feel lonely. Perhaps not well'. It seems that she was trying to describe some deep malaise she did not understand. Like Joseph Hardie, the hard life was causing her to 'lose her health'. She had been a strong and vital woman, working beside her husband on the farm, and coping alone if he went away. She cared for her children, milked and made her butter, often rising early in the morning on hot summer days to get it done before the heat, selling some to Tait and Co., and the rest to local shop-keepers and neighbours. She prided herself on her lack of idleness, and her worst trouble seemed to be toothache. But on 14 July she noted, 'I have not been well all day I think or else very lazy', and the next day she was 'not at all well'.

She worried about her children, and it was Bert who was having the hardest time of it.

3.6   *Poor little Bertie had quite an adventure coming from school tonight, an old Bear caught him by the Leg as he was passing him, he says that he had to hit him with his bare hand and he did not know what to do. He was nearly heart broken when he came home but he says he did not let the bear see him crying.*

This experience put Bert off going to school, and on 18 July he was frightened by a story at school of a boy being eaten by a wild dog. On 6 August John was suffering from bad toothache, and Catherine's frustration spilled out after a visit from Mrs Atkinson and her children: 'we were never so tired of anyone. I do hope they will not come back'.

On 8 September, another hand wrote in the diary 'Went to town and stayed till Monday. John came home and went for Mother on Tues 13th'. On 14 September John wrote in the diary, 'I fill this up as mother is very ill'. Two days later Mr and Mrs McPherson, Mrs Hardie and Jane came to view the invalid, and John sent for the doctor at Warragul and was advised to send Catherine to town, as she 'cannot eat or sleep or take medicine'. Catherine was violent and destructive, and John needed the help of Mr Gregory and Mr McPherson to get her on the train in order to take her to Melbourne. She had to be restrained on the train, and she later remembered most bitterly that she had been tied up in a corn sack. Lizzie met the sad party in Melbourne, and they stayed overnight with Leaper Wells. The next day the brother and sister helped John take Catherine to be examined by Doctors Williams and Campbell. 'There is no doubt', said Doctor Campbell, 'that she is suffering from furious mania'. Doctor Williams noted that she 'speaks incoherently—informs me that her husband who is holding her is not her husband at all. She spat at me when I

85

asked her who he was'. Lizzie told the doctors that Catherine had been violent, and had not slept for four days and four nights. There was no doubt that Catherine would have to be committed, and John left her at the Yarra Bend Asylum.[43]

While he was in Melbourne, John took the opportunity of visiting the Land Office, and he left for home on 19 September. He immediately began selling oats to keep his mind off his troubles, but noted gloomily on 20 September, 'All the women on the road was out. Showing what estimation mother is held in. I wish she was better'. John now took over the diary, and the normally taciturn farmer filled its pages with an outpouring of anguish and guilt. Maybe he was using the book as a way of communicating with Catherine, hoping that she would read it and know of his feelings, for his recurring theme was his inability to tell her of his love. On 26 September he 'got a letter from Mrs Wells saying how dear old Kate is a deal better. I am so thankful as we are such a helpless lot without her'. In October he travelled to Melbourne to visit her.

1.10   *Went and saw dear old Kate. She looks very bad but is very sensible. Had a long confab, stopped till they gave me the hint to go away. What an establishment. But my very heart is sore as I come home to leave poor mother there.*

On 5 October John got a letter from the Master in Lunacy, and the next day a letter from Lizzie saying that Catherine was getting on 'first rate'. The children all sat down to write to her.

On 9 October John received a good report from Melbourne, and recorded,

'the sins of the Fathers unto the third and fourth Generation'. Went to McPhersons but they had heard the good news. For it is good to

*everyone hereabouts as my wife is respected by everybody . . . Oh if
she had but trusted me just a little more this terrible calamity
would not have happened.*

A letter arrived from Catherine telling of her troubles, and John
reflected on his failings.

14.10 *Poor martar she punished herself to save me trouble, oh had she
only talked her troubles over they would have been nothing.*

    . . .

19.10 *Still the yearning. If Mother had told me about Ann all would
have been well—to save me an unpleasant thought she almost
killed herself. I think she should have known me better but I
behaved badly to her. A man that is too proud to let a wife know
how he loves her will get punished.*

    . . .

20.10 *It is near the anniversary of the child's death and I am frightened
for that time. All that I have talked to seems to think that we made
a mistake in not talking it over quietly.*

Catherine was still 'not so well a little excited and restless'. The doctor
suggested that John should not visit for a while, as seeing him upset
her. He went back to his work on the farm, scarcely mentioning the
children. One wonders about Bert's nightmares of bears, and whether
anyone was comforting him. On 31 October some leases arrived for
John, and he put them in the bank for safe keeping. At the end of the
month John had letters from Dr Griffiths and Lizzie, saying that
Catherine was no worse, but had shown no positive improvement. He
thought back on past mistakes: 'was ever teasing her. I thought she
liked it'. A letter from Catherine on 4 November prompted him to
more self-recrimination; 'she tried to keep the wind from blowing on

me and caught it herself she says', and five days later, 'oh my dear if you had only trusted me and I had not been so proud . . . I trusted too much to myself and have proved a rotten reed'. On 10 November John went once more to Melbourne, and came home again with a bad cold: 'if mother had only been here she would have nursed me', he complained.

On 14 November he reflected, ' "May God be merciful". Oh had she but trusted me. What a monster I appear.' The next day he thought 'If she only gets fair play she will soon be well but she is at the mercy and caprice of the nurses.' He got some 'rambling' letters from Mother, and caught another cold. Bertie was also sick and John wrote to Lizzie to see if she would 'come and look after us', but Lizzie, presumably thinking that Catherine's needs were greater, did not reply. A letter came from Mrs Wells to say that Catherine was a great deal better, and that her 'bad turns' did not last so long. On 29 November Jane arrived to stay for two days, and John felt rather better. But in December another letter upset him.

10.12   *Mother is speaking of not writing as I will not come for her. Poor myrtar she tried to save me and killed herself, oh how I blame myself. I have been so selfish I will never forgive myself.*

12.12   *Mrs. Hardie here ye ken. She hardly asked for Mother. I could kick her.*

Allied to John's recriminations was a growing worry about the effect of Catherine's madness on her status in the community. Often the ladies were not at home as he passed, and those he saw avoided the subject of his wife's illness. His diary entries constantly and defensively returned to the respect in which Catherine was held in the district. To add to his troubles, it was not only John who was blaming himself for Catherine's state.

18.12   *My own wife how my heart bleeds for her and I was the cause. I was so selfish and made her afraid of me then she could not trust me.*

19.12   *Letter from Mrs. Wells and a most complete rebuke or lecture. I never got such a sore one in all my life. May she never be in the same trouble to need comfort and advice as I have been, but I have gone through so far and I must trust to my Father in heaven for earthly friends is hard upon me. . . .*

21.12   *I must try to study mother better as she has a very sensitive disposition oh had she trusted me.*

On Christmas Day, John noted dolefully, 'the first time for 17 Years that we have not had Mother to get her dinner'.

On 27 December John left for Melbourne, and the next day made formal demand for the release of Catherine. 'Mother was fine all the way home' he noted, as he and Lizzie brought her home on the train.

1882

On New Year's Day 1882 Jane came to visit, and John noted that it excited Catherine just a little, and that Jane was looking stout. The next day Mother was 'not so well and quarrelsome', but by 8 January John was recording the 'difference in the comfort' now that Catherine was home. The next week Catherine took up her pen again, with little reference to the experience of the past months, and by 19 January was once more out in the paddocks, piling the wheat into small loads. By the 24 January, after some late mornings, Catherine was feeling fine, and had enough energy to note that Syme had come to dinner and was 'telling Lies I thought, and giving *cheek*'. On 26 January Mr Sergeant came to witness a transfer of land, and the next day John got a letter from Mrs Steadman with a very *welcome enclosure*.

At the beginning of February Lizzie went home, obviously thinking that Catherine was able to cope. The threshing machine arrived, and the Curries had 119 bags of good oats. But in the middle of the month the fires began again, and Rintel's store was burnt down. Bert was having trouble with the Syme children, who would not let him cross their selection. Daffy the horse died, probably of snake bite, and the February blues struck again. There would be no slow and peaceful recovery for Catherine.

In March the rain came and life became more pleasant. On 31 March John took James to Mr Sargent 'to sign a paper that he had never been insolvent'. It is possible that John was transferring James's land. John took Catherine to the show, and on Good Friday put up a merry-go-round for the children. Catherine's sister Carrie came to stay, and to help Jane, who had a new daughter in April. Bertie cut one foot on the merry-go-round in April, and damaged the other one with an axe in May. Catherine noted, 'Bertie went to school. He has been this fortnight with his sore feet. I had to carry him nearly all the way' [15.5]. John nominated for the council in July, and Catherine had high hopes, but at the election in August he came 'lowest in the poll'. The work of the farm continued, and in September Catherine complained of feeling sick after she had worked all day cleaning oats and helping to lift some bags. On 30 September, nine months after returning from the Asylum, and four months after carrying the six-year-old Bertie to school, Catherine gave birth to a daughter Carolyn Calphurnia. Named after her aunt, and the ship that had brought her mother's family to Australia thirty-seven years before her birth, she was known to the family as Fern. Jane came with her new baby to help out for a couple of days.

The relationship with the Cunninghams was uneasy. On 8 October Catherine remarked that Jane was insulted when she would not let Katie go to mind Jane's place while she was away, and later in the month 'Neil here to dinner but I did not get a word with him'. But the ever dependable Lizzie arrived in November, bringing her sewing machine to make dresses for Catherine and Katie and pinafores for the new baby. Catherine still had her low days; she had had swollen legs since the birth of the baby, and sometimes wondered 'Shall I ever be quite strong again'. But on Boxing Day her sister Carrie was married, and she and her new husband Harry arrived on 29 December to spend New Year's Eve. Catherine noted that they had a merry evening. Maybe life would get back to normal again.

Madness

The people clearing the forests of Gippsland were among the last of the Australian pioneers, and they were conscious that they were heirs to a great tradition. Catherine Currie hated to think that one of her sons would do less work than any other man, for the true pioneer was a strong and noble workman, capable of prodigious efforts that would amaze those city folk immortalised by the poet only for 'their stunted forms and weedy'. Pioneers, men and women alike, could cope with heat and rain, isolation and hardship, for they had sound minds in healthy bodies. One of the Gippsland pioneers noted in his reminiscences that in the early days of hard work in the forests no one ever went mad.[44] It was an important point for him to make, for it indicated the superiority of the pioneers and their pristine environment.

By the nineteenth century the scientific literature on insanity suggested that madness could be a disease of physical origin, but it was still thought that it was largely a result of environment. In the eighteenth century insanity had been generally seen to be related to dramatic social change. When the world became 'disordered', it was likely that the more fragile minds would follow suit. In France, Phillippe Pinel showed that the French Revolution had produced an increase in psychoses, and other European and American studies demonstrated a similar causal relationship between revolution and mental disturbance. The theory persisted, and its corollary was that a stable and ordered society produced stable and sane citizens. The assessment of the number of insane was a measure of the success of a society. Madness, its presence or absence, was an indicator of civilisation. As the insane were gathered into asylums through the eighteenth and nineteenth centuries, it was possible for the medical profession to collect statistics and carry out more scientific surveys. Through the nineteenth century, debate raged on the role of social change, environment and ethnic origin in the incidence of insanity.[45]

In 1873 the English researcher Edgar Sheppard completed a statistical profile to show that insanity occurred most frequently between the ages of thirty and forty, was more frequent in summer than in winter, and among agricultural rather than town populations—a profile that fitted Catherine Currie rather nicely. The fact that there was more lunacy in the country than in towns puzzled Sheppard, for it seemed to him that 'The vices and wear and tear of great cities, with all the attendant evils of dense gregariousness, would seem to invite disease in a larger ratio than in the country.'[46] He decided that factors contributing to the opposite case were that people in the country were worse fed and they did not have as much intellectual stimulation.

Environmental theories made it important to decide whether insanity was more prevalent in the city or in the country, and American scholars began to collect information on their frontier. After A. O. Wright conducted a survey in Wisconsin in 1881, he presented his results to the National Conference of Charities and Correction in 1884:

Having made a census of the insane under public care in Wisconsin, the writer, on reducing the number by counties to the ratio to the population of the several counties, was astonished to find here a general law; that the older settled counties had the largest ratio of insane to the population, and that the ratio steadily decreased and reached the smallest ratio in the pioneer counties on the north. This seemed to show that a new country has a smaller proportion of insanity than an old country.[47]

This, he thought, was probably because pioneering people were of a certain age group and were fit and healthy. He added in his report, 'It is often claimed that insanity is a disease of civilization, and that it is increasing because civilization is increasing. This I think to be a mistake.' In a study in 1887, Judson B. Andrews agreed that the figures showed that

> the pioneers of our newer settlements are the more hardy and vigorous citizens, and that the feeble and dependent are left in their former homes, to enjoy the comforts of the hospitals and asylums, which are the special growth of the older civilization.[48]

The debate on madness and civilisation was important in Australia. A country that had grown from a penal colony was now intent on evolving towards higher status and culture. Experts took up the discussion of the role played by environment in the moral 'deterioration of nature', and added to the ethos of the strong and healthy bush worker which was already being expressed in literature and in poems like *Faces in the Street* and *Clancy of the Overflow*. In the *Australasian Medical Gazette* of December 1883, Doctor Maudsley suggested that many ill effects sprang from 'the conditions of our present civilization', and the pursuit of wealth. It was generally agreed that 'morbid emotional states' were more common among less cultured people, but it was true that cities produced pressures that would not only lead to personal deterioration, but to the degeneration of the family:

It is not that the fluctuations of excitement unhinge the merchant's mind, and lead to maniacal outbreaks, although that does sometimes happen; it is not that failure in the paroxysm of some crisis prostrates his energies and makes him melancholic, although that also is occasionally witnessed; but it is that the exclusiveness of his life's aim and occupation too often saps the moral element in his nature, makes him egotistic, formal, and unsympathetic, and, in his person, deteriorates the nature of humanity. What is the consequence?

If one conviction has been fixed in my mind more distinctly than another, by observation of instances, it is that it is extremely unlikely such a man will beget healthy children; on the contrary, it is extremely likely that the deterioration of nature, which he has acquired, will be transmitted as an evil heritage to his children.

In several instances in which the father has toiled upwards from poverty to vast wealth, with the aim and hope of founding a family, I have witnessed the results in a degeneracy—mental and physical—of his offspring, which has sometimes gone as far as extinction of the family in the 3rd or 4th generation.[49]

Perhaps the worst fate that could be imagined for Catherine Currie was for her to go violently and indisputably mad. There were some perfectly sane reasons for this respectable pioneer woman to lose her grip on her sanity. She lived in the middle of a wild and threatening environment, and was seasonally ringed by raging bushfires that terrified her. She was married to a man who did not willingly take advice or encourage confidences or self-pity, and she had no close friend with whom to share her troubles. She was a woman who was filled with longings for a wealth and status she would never attain; she was a woman of intelligence and ambition who watched her more retiring husband take on the public roles in church and community which she herself may have been fitted for, had she been born in another generation. All her energies were channelled into being the perfect mother, for this was the only course of excellence available to her. Eventually she failed even at that. Her beloved baby, whose welfare was her sole responsibility, drowned in a well while her back was turned.

On a personal level there was sympathy for Catherine. Her husband John blamed himself for his lack of insight and concern. The children missed their mother and neighbours rallied round when she returned from the asylum. But this episode was not as easy to cope with as physical illness. John noted that no neighbours came to greet him as he returned from the first sad trip to Melbourne, and that few asked after his wife. There was an unease about mental illness, an unspoken censure of which Catherine would always remain aware, a feeling that she had forfeited her natural place in society, a feeling of moral failure. Catherine's tragedy was not only a personal and individual failure, but a crime against her family, community and society. In her ordered society there was a terror of anything that raged out of control, whether it was bushfires or human emotions. To become a lunatic was to become 'disordered' in a society that prized progress and order above all things. To go mad was to move outside the pale of civilisation and lose all claim to respectability and status. Catherine Currie had not only failed to live up to the promise of her hardy pioneering forebears, but she had brought shame to her country and her family.

Catherine was admitted to Melbourne's Yarra Bend Asylum in 1881, the year of the census. The statistics recorded her as being of English birth, but she added one more to the Victorian total. Each colony anxiously compared the figures with those of other colonies and with the older countries of Europe. The 1881 census was not particularly reassuring; the *Victorian Year Book* for 1884–85 showed that in 1861 there had been one lunatic for every 819 persons, but by 1881 the figure stood at one in every 304. The Colonial Statistician stated sadly,

From whatever cause, lunacy appears to be much more rife in Victoria than in England and Wales. When the census of 1881 was take, the proportion in the latter was 1 lunatic in every 502 of the population, which is a much lower proportion than that found to exist in Victoria in the same census.[50]

Ephraim Zox, who from 1884 to 1886 headed a royal commission into Victorian asylums, remarked that the 1883 figures on madness put the colony in 'the most unenviable position of being the maddest place in the world'.[51]

By the 1880s the asylum statistics recorded that the large majority of patients were suffering physical rather than moral problems.[52] But the stigma of moral and perhaps social depravity remained and, after the 1881 census, commentators went to some lengths to defend the Australian moral fibre by maintaining that there was a greater amount of insanity among foreign-born than native-born Australian people. Doctor Manning, Inspector-General of the Insane in New South Wales, noted that in New South Wales in 1881 the proportion of insane per 1000 people was 8.03 for British-born, 6.87 for other foreign-born, and only 1.22 for Australian-born. He qualified these proud statistics to some extent:

The comparatively small proportion of insanity among Australians is partly to be accounted for by the fact that fully one-third of these are children, whilst insanity is mainly a disease of middle life and old age, but there are some reasons which I have not time to detail, which lead to the pleasant conclusion that Australians are less subject to insanity than people of other races living in Australia.[53]

The stigma of going mad was worsened by the fact that the insane had long been grouped with common criminals as people to be locked away for the safety of the respectable and law-abiding citizens. In

Australia, as elsewhere in the world, the mad were incarcerated in prisons until the nineteenth century, when doctors and others began a campaign to have insanity viewed as a physical disease rather than moral degeneration. The first Australian asylum was built at Tarban Creek in New South Wales in 1838, and a few of the more dangerous and uncontrollable patients from the Port Phillip District were sent by ship to this asylum, later to be known as Gladesville. The transportation of lunatics, remarks Charles Brothers, afforded the people of Melbourne much entertainment, 'such events invariably being highlighted in the Port Phillip Gazette'.[54] Most of the colony's lunatics, however, were kept in the watchhouse of the Collins Street gaol, disturbing the passing populace with their 'maniacal yells and laughter'.

In 1845 the New South Wales government called for tenders for an asylum to be built near Melbourne. On 11 August 1848 the *Argus* reported: 'A site of 620 acres has been selected for the establishment of a new Lunatic Asylum at the junction of the Merri Creek and Yarra River, adjoining the aboriginal ground reserve at Dight's Mills'. The bluestone building was opened in October 1848, and was officially known as the Lunatic Asylum Merri Creek, or the Melbourne Asylum.

The original building was designed on the lines of a prison, with separate wards for male and female inmates, smaller cells for intractable or dangerous patients, and airing courts to allow supervised exercise and a controlled intake of fresh air. The theory was that patients should be removed from the environment that had caused their madness, and be placed in an ordered and peaceful environment. The building reflected this desire for order for it was straight and regimented, with separate compartments for different functions.

In practice, however, there was little peace and tranquillity. The original building was soon fully occupied, and a new wing was completed in 1850. After the separation of the colony from New South Wales in 1851, the Victorian asylum became known as Yarra Bend.

From the beginning there was controversy about the asylum and its management. Commentators could not even agree on the nature of the site: some contemporary observers saw it as an unhealthy bog, and to others it seemed a place to rival the Botanical Gardens, a place of rest and beauty where the mad could recuperate in a peaceful environment. There was little peace inside the walls, however, for from the beginning the asylum provided inadequate and over-crowded accommodation, and the population explosion of the gold-rush period ensured that the resources of staff and buildings would be stretched to their limits. The grounds began to resemble a camp site rather than a prison, with a collection of smaller buildings and even tents scattered around the original bluestone building.

The first superintendents of the Australian asylums were appointed for political reasons. They were not qualified medical men, but were seen as managers and warders of the insane rather than as men attempting to cure patients. The first superintendent at Yarra Bend established a pig and poultry farm on the site, using the labour of the patients for his own financial benefit. In 1852 a committee of enquiry found that the attendants, some of whom were inmates themselves, were guilty of 'immoral conduct', and condemned the coercion and punishment of inmates by such means as shower baths used as 'engines of torture'. In 1858 another committee of enquiry formally approved the already existing 'cottage system', with non-violent patients accommodated away from the main wards. Within the walls the inmates worked as farm or garden labourers, in the sewing room, kitchen or laundry.

The many select committees and enquiries kept the problem of madness at the forefront of the community's consciousness. The deprivation of liberty was a major punishment, and by the time Catherine Currie was admitted on 17 September 1881 there were strict laws and regulations to govern admission to a Victorian asylum.

Bundled up in a corn sack, deprived of her freedom and dignity, Catherine had been brought by train to Melbourne, where her sister Lizzie met them and helped John to take her to Yarra Bend. There was no doubt that she was violently mad, but her rights still had to be protected. The Lunacy Acts of the Australian colonies followed British precedent, and according to law John signed an order requesting the Superintendent, Doctor Paley, to admit his wife to the asylum. In Victoria, two medical certificates from independent doctors were required before a patient could be admitted to an asylum at the request of a relative or friend. The medical officer was required to give a separate certificate of insanity after admission. There was provision for inspection by commissioners, inspectors and official visitors while the patient was detained in the asylum.

John supplied the necessary personal details in the admission form. He stated that this was his wife's first attack of madness, and that the suspected cause was the death of her child by drowning. He reported the duration of the attack as seven or eight months, although it was listed on later records as seven or eight weeks. He stated that the reason that the patient had not been examined before being brought to Yarra Bend was that her residence was 'so far from any medical men'. Two doctors examined Catherine at Yarra Bend and supplied medical certificates to confirm that she was insane and violent. Doctor Campbell concluded that there was no doubt 'but that she is suffering from furious mania', and Doctor Williams agreed that she was destructive and suffering from insomnia.

John and Lizzie left Catherine in the care of the doctors, and once they had gone some of the details of her records became a little confused. The admission book reported that Catherine was suffering from mania, and that her bodily condition was delicate. The case book of the asylum noted that she was not suicidal or epileptic, but that she was strong and healthy, dangerous and destructive:

Hands and wrists swolen from tying.

This woman is strong and robust in person and appears healthy. She suffers from acute mania and is very violent and dangerous. She refuses her food and is in all respects difficult to manage.[55]

There were some discrepancies in the records. The person who filled in the case-book gave her age as thirty rather than thirty-six, did not know her family details, habits of life, native place, whether she had had any previous attacks, or whether the condition was hereditary. No doubt the attendants were too busy dealing with their destructive patient to read the warrant filled in by John and Lizzie. There is no account of the treatment Catherine was given, but within a month the case-book recorded that 'Since admission this woman has much improved and is now fairly well'.

At the time Catherine Currie was admitted to Yarra Bend, the treatment for her common condition of mania seemed to be one of reasonably benign *laissez-faire*. The early nineteenth-century idea that madness was a moral and environmental problem had led to the simple notion that the patient should be removed from the surroundings that had caused the problem, and be given fresh air, exercise, hard work and moral instruction.[56] In Victoria in 1881 this formula was still followed, although more medical men were beginning to question such unscientific practice. In November 1883, after Doctor Paley had retired from the asylum, he was criticised for his old-fashioned approach to the running of the Victorian asylums:

For upwards of twenty years, and up to within a few months ago [the Victorian asylums] were directed by a gentleman who, judging him by the condition of the asylums under his care, and by the results of the treatment adopted, never took a genuinely scientific interest in his work ... he never regarded himself as, of necessity, the physician of a hospital containing patients, but only the superintendent of a place of detention, the inmates in which got well, or died, or left without getting well, as it might happen. He did not, as a matter of practice, subject them to systematic treatment. He was a kind-hearted, easy-going, amiable, gentlemanly sort of man, and what wonder, therefore, if those who served under him for the most part followed in his footsteps, and allowed things to take their course in the same *laissez-faire* fashion. The result has been that, with about half a dozen exceptions, the medical officers of the lunatic asylums of Victoria have taken no true interest in their duties. They have not been selected for any special competency; most of them have been young men fresh from their universities, having, in fact, everything to learn, and it must be confessed that no inducement has been held out to them to remain sufficiently long to enable them to acquire the special knowledge the possession of which should have been a condition of appointment.[57]

While the professionals railed against the lack of science and medical training, such amiable and non-intrusive treatment was probably the best thing for Catherine Currie. There were some means of restraint available to the attendants; difficult or dangerous patients were kept in Ward B while they were violent, and could be restrained by means of the camisole, or straight-jacket, locked gloves and webbed petticoats. There were strict regulations governing the use of such restraint, which had to be recorded in the case-book, and by the end of the 1880s it was reported that restraint was used on average only in one out of three or four hundred cases.[58] As had been the case thirty years earlier, there were strict rules to prevent the shower bath being used as an instrument of punishment. Those who refused to eat could be fed by tube through the nostrils. There is no record of any of these measures being used in the Currie case. The favoured treatment was fresh air and exercise, a good diet and plenty of sleep, if necessary induced by a sedative such as chloral hydrate. Once the patient became quieter, she was sent to live in one of the cottages outside the main building, and worked at various domestic tasks. Such occupational therapy would no doubt have made the hard-working Catherine Currie feel more at home.

The attendants were used to dealing with cases like Catherine's, for mania was the most prevalent diagnosis for people presenting at the lunatic asylums in the late nineteenth century. In 1801 Philippe Pinel had defined mania as 'excessive nervous excitement with or without delerium', and others described it as 'raving madness', accompanied by deranged understanding and the incoherence of ideas. Jerzy Krupinski and Lynn Alexander suggest that while in the mid-nineteenth century mania was diagnosed for 60 per cent of female patients, today only about 2.5 per cent of these cases would receive the same diagnosis.[59] What was diagnosed in the nineteenth century as dementia praecox or delusional insanity would now be called schizophrenia, melancholia would be known as depressive illness, and idiocy called mental retardation.

On 27 December 1881 Catherine's case-book noted that she could leave the asylum: 'Allowed on trial till 31st January 1882 under the Care of her Husband'. The Currie diary recorded that John left for Melbourne on 27 December to collect his wife and bring her home again. She would not join the statistics of the 'recovered' until after she had been certified sane by a medical practitioner. According to both the Discharge Register and her case-book, Catherine Currie was officially discharged from Yarra Bend on 27 October 1883. Dr Manning reported that the recovery rate in Australian asylums for the decennial period 1878 to 1887 was 42.09 per cent, compared with the English rate of 40.04 per cent, and a recovery rate below 40 per cent in Scotland and Ireland for the same period. He added: 'It should be noted, however, that whilst the statistics of Australian asylums include idiots—a very incurable class—these are eliminated from the English statistics, and the Australian returns are therefore even better than they would at first sight appear'.[60]

Catherine was just happy to be home again. She picked up the threads of her life, trying to ignore the Yarra Bend experience until two years later, when in October 1883 she was sent for by the local doctor who gave her her final certificate of discharge. For some time there are no reports in the diary of further breakdowns, although Catherine reports headaches and anxiety throughout the following years. The experience of Yarra Bend is not mentioned in the diary until January 1894, when the whole dreadful episode is recalled, and blamed for the lack of respect shown to her by children and husband. In October 1895, after a trip away from home, the unspeakable happened, and on 9 December the terrible performance began once more, with Catherine being admitted to Yarra Bend suffering from 'delusional insanity'.

This time, it seemed, John was not sympathetic, and far from taking the blame for her condition, distanced himself from this latest episode. It was Bert who took his mother to the Railway Hotel in Drouin to be examined by the doctors. Two medical certificates were forwarded to Melbourne, each following a set formula. Doctor Geoffrey Travers reported:

I the undersigned being a Medical Practitioner hereby certify that I on the ninth day of December One Thousand eight hundred and ninety five at Leith's Hotel Drouin (Main Street) in the county of Buln Buln, separately from any other Medical Practitioner personally examined Sarah Ann Catherine Currie of Drouin and that the said Sarah Ann Catherine Currie is a lunatic and a proper person to be taken charge of and detained under care and treatment and that I have formed this opinion upon the following grounds. Viz.

(1) Facts indicating insanity observed by myself: Is under the delusion that her children are better than other people's, and that they will be stolen—Says that 'mischievous fingers' are upon her.

(2) Other facts indicating insanity communicated by others: Patient's son Albert Bryce Currie tells me that his mother is destructive and inclined to break furniture. That she has not slept properly lately.

His colleague Doctor Robert Smith concurred:

I the undersigned being a Medical Practitioner hereby certify that on the 9th day of December 1895 at Drouin at Leith's Railway Hotel Main Street in the County of Buln Buln, separately from any other medical practitioner, personally examined Sarah Ann Catherine Currie of Drouin and that the said Sarah Ann Catherine Currie is a lunatic and a proper person to be taken charge of and detained under care and treatment and that I have formed this opinion upon the following facts namely

First. Facts indicating insanity observed by myself. *Personal disorder of hair and dress. destructiveness.* delusions as to persons of her acquaintance.

Second. Other facts indicating insanity communicated to me by others.

Destructive. Insomnia. by Albert Currie (Son).

This time it was Catherine's brother who took her to Yarra Bend and signed the order requesting that she be admitted once more to the asylum. She was now fifty years old, and the children she was afraid would be stolen were aged between twenty-seven and eleven. Doctor Watkins, the new Superintendent at Yarra Bend, admitted Catherine for her second stay. The Admission Register noted that she had been 'disordered' before, and that the duration of the present attack was two months. There was no cause given for her attack, and her health was noted as robust. The notes made in her case-book said: 'Suffering from mania. Stubborn and disobedient. Sent to B Ward. In fair bodily health—not a very good sleeper. H:Chld when required'. In February 1896 she was discharged on probation leave with her husband, and in July was noted as officially discharged after receiving a certificate from Doctor Travers.

It is hard to know from the diary whether Catherine suffered any further attacks of 'lunacy'. It is obvious that she was bitter, conscious of disgrace and failure, and that she attributed most of her subsequent difficulties with her husband and children to the fact that she had twice been sent to the asylum. The vibrant optimism had gone, and the sharp wit had now degenerated into jealousy and self-pity.

Catherine Currie lived in a time and place when a woman's role was clearly defined. It was her responsibility to be a good wife and mother. Even in a pioneering family, where a woman took her part in the work of the farm, the production of butter, the clearing of trees, planting of gardens and digging of wells, her first responsibility was still to husband and children. The world made by men did not allow much room for manoeuvre. Catherine had come to her new and difficult home with hope and ambition, and even when she saw the tiny clearing in the impenetrable bush, she had seen the possibilities and liked it well. But by 1881 she had failed in the things she most valued—to be a respected member of the community, to be a firm and good mother, to be a supportive wife. She had been driven mad and committed to an insane asylum perceived as a prison for common criminals, drunkards and idiots. She found herself in the place described by Ephraim Zox as a 'rubbish bin' of caste-off humanity.[61] The landscape of her life had been permanently changed.

There was a place for eccentricity in the pioneer legend, but the pioneer of legend was generally masculine. The old shepherd who sat in his isolated hut mumbling to himself and the kangaroos could be accommodated. But women were the bearers of civilisation as well as the next generation of hardy Australians. There was no place in the

legend for a woman who spat at doctors, destroyed furniture, dis-
owned her husband and was 'disordered' in hair and dress. Catherine
Currie had irrevocably forfeited her place in the legend, and she knew
it well. She lived the rest of her life with blighted hopes, still pining
for a nice house and good singing as a sign that she was worthy of a
cultured and civilised life. She lived with the thought that her husband
and children no longer respected her.

There were many good reasons for Catherine Currie to go violently
mad, but there were other women in similar positions who did not.
Other women lived hard and isolated lives, watched their children die,
fought fire or flood or drought, and did not go mad. But Catherine was
isolated in other ways, because of her personality. There is no doubt
that she was a difficult person to live with, both for her family and herself. She was stubborn and dominating, quick to take offence and
jealous of her position. She lived in a community which provided
many avenues for social pleasures and friendly gatherings, and yet she
was insular and had no close friends. She fought with her family, and
found it hard to talk to her husband. She attempted always to domi-
nate her children, with much success until they grew old enough to
discuss their mother's madness and its significance for their own lives.

Contemporary local wisdom says that the children of Catherine
Currie had made a pact not to marry, for presumably they had a good
understanding of animal and plant breeding, and perhaps also the
laws of evolution, and were aware that there could be a flaw that
should not be allowed to be passed on, in the interests of the survival
of the fittest. The mother now carried the 'evil heritage' which could
be transmitted to her children as an acquired 'deterioration of nature'.
Catherine and her madness had forced a pause, a discontinuity in the
narrative of family progress.

Catherine's madness broke the dialogue between herself and other
people. She had never been very good at communicating in the spoken

word, but at least she had known her place and her role, which gave her the correct language to deal with the world, even on the borders of ambiguity. Now that madness had broken down her inhibitions and made her utter words unfit for a woman in her position, her role was no longer clear. For a short time the diary was silent, and when it began again it was as monologue rather than as dialogue.

Michel Foucault has said that the act of categorising madness as a disease brought about a silence, and broke the dialogue between reason and madness which had occurred in previous times:

> This dialogue itself was now disengaged; silence was absolute; there was no longer any common language between madness and reason; the language of delirium can be answered only by an absence of language, for delirium is not a fragment of dialogue with reason, it is not a language at all; it refers, in an ultimately silent awareness, only to transgression.[62]

The language of psychiatry, says Foucault, is a monologue of reason *about* madness, and has been established only on the basis of this silence.[63] Catherine's madness was a twist of the plot she had never considered when she began her diary. Someone had moved the props that held up the sky, and the narrative had been disrupted, disconnected at its source. When Catherine returned home again, she took up her pen once more. But now it was with awareness of transgression.

Yuulong 1883–1893

Life had to go on much as before, as the diary testified. The years were still filled with the seasonal work of the farm, and the expanding social life of the children. But Catherine's life had closed in, and much of her energy and exuberance of former years was missing. The optimistic hopes with which Catherine and John came to their new life had dissipated, for not only had the farm failed to fulfil initial expectations, but Catherine herself was now no longer the strong, decent and respectable farmer's wife she had once been, at least in her own eyes. The work that was once a sign of her worth had become merely a burden, one that was often too heavy for her. Catherine's anxiety and pessimism extended also to her relations with her husband and children. In spite of John's good intentions and resolutions, the diary indicates that never again would Catherine and John feel quite the same about each other, and Catherine would from this time always doubt the children's respect for her. Other close relationships were also dissolved, through death or disagreement.

1883

In January 1883 James disappeared, and the neighbours rallied to search for him. Catherine's concern was more for John than James.

John was exhausted after searching for James, but went out to cradle the oats in the afternoon. This life, said Catherine, was 'nothing but trouble, everything fighting against one. I am so anxious for Daa himself for fear he gets laid up'. She also feared for herself, and on 19 January she wrote, 'I feel as if it was not much trying to live. It seems such a struggle and I do try to do right'. Catherine was now sending her butter to Mr Tait, and negotiating for him to take the Cunningham's produce as well, although she decided to save her sister's pride by concealing the fact from her. Despite all that had happened, she was still trying to influence and manipulate other people's lives.

4.2   *Daa drove Baby Bert and I up to Woodene, took them quite by surprise but I had to see about their butter. Tait sent me word that they would take it on account of us, but I did not tell them so.*

In February it was fires as usual, and Jane came to tell the Curries that Neil had sold his place for £4 an acre. Jane was not happy, as she would have liked to live in the house they had just finished building. In March John lit a fire that ran out of control. It burnt Hardie's fence, and it took a great fight to save their house. Mrs Hardie came to speak to John, and Catherine recorded the conversation.

9.3   *She came over in the evening to say that he could take the saplings off her ground to put up his own fence after her fence was made. She just came on the impulse ye ken. I am so impulsive but I thought I should send for Bob Gregory and have a right fence made, when ye was at it. I told her it would be a right fence when Mr. Currie was done with it, the impudence of the old thing, but John says it is ignorance.*

Later in the month John shot a little creature that had been eating the apples, and they took it to Logies Lodge the next day, where it was identified as a flying fox. The Curries handed it over to grandfather

Hardie, who wanted to stuff it, and when they later shot another one, they had it stuffed for themselves. The weather improved, and Catherine described one beautiful sunny day as 'like old country May', probably more from hearsay than remembrance. She was still making judgements about people, and when R. Hamilton came for tea on 13 May she confided to her diary, 'I don't like him at all, he is not a good man'.

In June a letter came from Jane to say the family had moved to Warragul, and when Neil called later Catherine tried to make him take some apples for Jane and the children, 'but he would not, almost threw them at me'. The children were not behaving well—Bert had been whipped and sent to bed in May and Fernie (aged only nine months) had her first whipping in June. In August Lachlan Grant lost his little girl with diphtheria, and this brought back sad memories for Catherine.

In October Catherine recorded bitterly,

13.10   *Mr. Byrne sent word by Tom yesterday that he wanted to see him—he wanted to ask him if it was* me *that had been shut up in Yarra Bend. Shall I ever here the last of the place. Oh why did they take* me *there.*

On 23 October Catherine was examined by the doctor 'for a certificate from the YBA his fee was half Guinea—I hope I am clear of them now'.

1884

The 1884 picnic was a success, and everybody liked Catherine's doughnuts, she recorded with pride. In March a letter came from E. Steadman to say the cottage in Scotland had been sold to

T. McGonigal for £142. Catherine was cheerful about the first sale of her fruit, for she hoped 'to get a chest of Drawers this year out the garden'. One of the last dreams to fade was the hankering for a more elegant house and furniture. Some of her social aspirations were now transferred to Katie, who had turned seventeen. Tom and Katie were invited to dances and parties, and Catherine sewed dresses for Katie to wear and invited neighbouring children to visit.

Other neighbours and members of the family were not in a happy state. On 15 April Tom went to Woodene, and Catherine noted, 'may not have to go there very much more, as they will be leaving soon'. Mrs Hardie was trying to sell some land, and came to tell the Curries that she had an offer of £2 5s per acre. Katie and Bert went to visit Mr McPherson, and heard that Sandy was off to the Snowy River to peg out some land. In April James, now aged sixty-two, became ill.

20.4   *We are very anxious all day about James Currie. He will not move today or take anything to eat or speak to say what is the matter with him. I can think of nothing else and I am sure John is thinking too what a trial he is to us.*

21.4   *We have been about nearly all night. John went to see if he could get James to speak to him in the evening—he took a drink of tea. John would have went for the Dr. but I would not let him. He James died about midnight. Daa went to Drouin to report the case to the police. Had to go to Warragul and the policeman came here.*

23.4   *Funeral. There were a good many attended the funeral out of respect for John I suppose as James was not known.*

24.4   *I am oh so tired tonight. I don't think ever I was so tired before and my work not done—as I must print my butter tonight yet.*

Jane was in very low spirits also, and on 26 April the Woodene sale was held.

On 21 May Catherine wrote to Lizzie asking her to come, and four days later a new daughter, Rose, was born. Lizzie had not come, and Catherine was annoyed: 'I dare say she was very sorry but I think she should have made some arrangements for me before'. On 17 June Catherine noted with pride that Bert had won prizes at school for geography and general knowledge, but on 20 June she was displeased with Neil, who promised much but did little, and by November it was John McEvoy who bore the brunt of her anger.

7.11   *John McEvoy got £1 10s cash he has not earned near that and he owed as much as that before he started and a bushel of oats since. I do not think Daa should have let him get it.*

1885

Many of Catherine's irritations and worries stemmed from the problem of money. She had to work hard for all she earned; in the heat of January 1885 she was often up at 3 a.m. to make butter before it became too hot. She was still sending her butter to Mr Tait, and complaining about the size of the cheques he was sending her:

4.5   *Letter and cheque from Mr. Tait. He is most indignant about my telling him about not give me the best Price for my butter. Says that whoever told me that he did not give me the highest price are Liars. My private opinion is that my letter helped the price this time as it rose 7d per lb in one week. It never rose as much as that before. Cheque for April £8 17s 9d.*

In February wallabies got into John's crop of oats, and Catherine noted, 'Daa says he will have no more oats till the vermin are fewer. One has no satisfaction at all'. Others in the district were also having trouble making ends meet, and Kenlock had tried to sell a piece of adjoining land to John, but the Curries could not afford it. In April Catherine recorded that Mrs Hardie had succeeded in selling a piece of her land.

In January John and Tom had gone to visit the new owners of Ireland's former selection, the Wilkinsons. Thomas and Annie Wilkinson had five children: Alice, Bruce, James (Jem) and Thomas. They called the property 'Hedley Hope', and Catherine remarked:

> *Tom says it is the prettiest place he ever saw but they did not go into the House as we have the whooping cough none of them spoke to Tom, is quite put out at being made so little of.*

No doubt the whooping cough was the cause, for Jem Wilkinson soon became Tom's best friend. In May Tom had his first dancing lesson at a party, and he and Katie went to dances at the Mechanics Hall. The children had now taken on a much larger role in the work of the farm, and Katie regularly did the milking. Catherine and Katie submitted entries for the Warragul Show: 'butter, bread, scones, bacon, hams, dog, shirt and socks', but Catherine recorded:

20.3   *Been all day at the show, such a long day. No more shows for me. Got no prizes, the prizes all went to friends of the committee.*

John was still involved in community affairs, and was secretary of the church committee. In August 1884 a new minister, Mr Lindt, had arrived, and the diary noted, 'they want the members of the committee to keep him week about, Mrs Hardie said she would take the first week of him'. Obviously such arrangements were not very attractive to the preacher, and Mr Lindt soon left, to be replaced by Mr McKay, whom

Catherine liked very much. But in March he was called to South Melbourne, a more attractive proposition than Lardner and, although the Curries went to church every Sunday, often there was no minister.

In June John was asked to stand for the council. In September he attended meetings to plan the building of a new Mechanics Institute Hall, and in October was arranging a transfer of land from J. J. Hamilton, who had promised to provide a site for the hall. In November there was a working party to chop logs, and by December John was helping to build the hall, and attending stormy meetings about when it should be opened.

> *G. Grant not pleased at us altering the date and Geo. Murdie not pleased at the contract being let without consulting him, but I think Daa does not mind any of them.*

Neil Cunningham was worrying Catherine in the second half of 1885, and she often recorded bad headaches after his visits. In November he brought John and Effie for Catherine to look after and in January the whole family, Neil, Jane and five children, came to stay. Catherine remarked that the house was very crowded, and on 14 January recorded:

> *Neil went off this morning . . . without breakfast bother him. I have been so cross. He never said he was going. Effie was complaining of a sore throat last night.*

The next day Neil took a house in Warragul and on 20 January 1886 'took off his Family. Did not even say thank you or good day even to anybody'. The Cunninghams disappeared from the farm and would now be mentioned only occasionally in Catherine's diary.

1886

February 1886 brought fires again, although they did not seem to bother Catherine quite as much as usual. John signed a contract to clear eleven acres for George Stoving on his neighbouring Yuulong property at £11 an acre. There was an election for the committee of the Mechanics Hall.

> *Daa told them he would not be Secretary unless they made him Treasurer as well, as he could not spare the time to be interviewing a Treasurer every time 5/– had to be paid.*

Mr Fraser was elected secretary, and Mr Hamilton treasurer, and then Mr Grant, arriving late from Buln Buln, 'told some of them they were upstarts so there was a Sort of General resignation—Daa is to get the entries of the Drouin institute and try and solder things up again'.

On Valentine's Day John received an unexpected gift, ten yards of tweed. Katie, filling in the diary for a few days, noted that it was 'such a surprise', and that no one could think who it had come from. In March the whole family was working on Stoving's clearing, and in March and April Catherine was ill, suffering from very bad headaches. In June there was more trouble with the new Mechanics Hall when, despite his promise, Hamilton refused to hand over the title to the land on which it had been built. John worried that the whole building would have to be moved, but Hamilton appeared to be relenting by September. On 14 September 1886 Catherine noted,

> *Bert came home a proud boy today, the Inspector at the School and Bert is to get a Sixth class certificate the only one of the school. The Master told them they all did well, we are all very pleased with Bert.*

On 17 September, Catherine 'bought the Sunday boots I promised him if he got the prize at School for Best Scholar.'

Such moments of pleasure and pride provided a brief respite from the hard work demanded by their own property. Now John had obtained some extra contract work at Yuulong, the property owned by Melbourne wool-broker George Stoving. In May 1885 Stoving had purchased the most westerly block of the original Hardie selection south of the Burnt Store Road, and the adjoining Rintel's corner. He now owned 640 acres of land opposite the Curries on Lardner's Track. Farmers were doing badly at this time, and although John had a bigger selection than most, he was looking for extra ways to support his family and his stock. In January 1887 Catherine complained, 'Daa says the grasshoppers have eaten all our grass—we must sell the other calves. It seems very hard on us will we ever be better'.

1887

Catherine's dreams of a peaceful and civilised life style seemed to be fading, and she was becoming more anxious and irritable. On 1 February 1887 she recorded:

> *we made a great mistake this morning and slept till 5 o'clock when Daa wanted to be up at 3.30 to catch the train to go and interview the ministers with a Deputation from Warragul. I am very sorry indeed as it is all my fault as Daa depended on me waking him. I have been worrying about it all day.*

Five days later she went to visit the Bairds, but it did not cheer her up: 'went to see the Bairds. The Bairds have a very nice House. I wish I had a house just like it but have given up hope of ever having one'. On 16 February J. J. Hamilton again refused to hand over the title to the Mechanics Hall land. Catherine's children were bothering her, and she noted in March, 'Bert was three hours away at the post . . . I must thrash him next time he is long, it looks bad to see boys idling'. In search of extra income, Catherine sent off a tender to carry the mails, and she signed a contract in April. She worried and had bad headaches about the new responsibility, for John was not keen on the idea, and Bert, who did the work, sometimes got lost and often complained.

In November 1887, the Cunninghams were mentioned again.

18.11   *Daa got a letter from Jane day before yesterday enclosing one I wrote Neil now nearly two years ago. She says he was very ill pleased at it, but I only told him he might have said thank you when he left. Anybody else would have paid for them and said thank you too—Daa did not read my letter and did not let me read Janes—he said it would only vex me for no good so he popped both into the fire. I give him credit for doing it but think if I ever meet Neil and am speaking to him I shall tell him just the same that was in the letter . . . I have a bad headache.*

Jane and John, loyal to their proud spouses, were no doubt united in the effort to calm troubled waters and keep the peace at home.

1888

Tom left the farm early in 1888 to seek work in Melbourne on the railways. He needed more remunerative work, but he was not happy with the sedentary work in the lamp room, and he returned home in

October. This was the first of many temporary departures, and Catherine was always unhappy when he went away. February of 1888 was also a bad month for fires, and Catherine and John fought about methods of controlling the risk.

28.2   *Daa thinks he should have burned yesterday but I did so wish him to wait till after the first March just for this time. He has always said he would wait and burned for this time and then said he wished he had waited. He is very angry with me as I advised him to wait. He thinks I do not care when God knows I try to think for the best way to save him. He asked for my reasons yesterday but when he gets in such a passion I get to frightened to speak but it does not seem right when one has always said they would wait to the first March and then never do it but I think he will wait this year now. How I hope it will be the best burn ever he had and I really think it will and perhaps not be very good at that as we never have had a good burn yet.*

Catherine was also beginning to record her increasingly frequent fights with Bert. She was late taking him his horse for the mail round in June, and 'he did scold'. In October Catherine went to Dandenong for a rare holiday, and was having such a good time that she wrote to say she would stay a few days longer than planned. Katie recorded 'Daa seems awfully put out about it thinks he will go down for her', and the next day Catherine was home to write in her diary that she had not had time to get any shopping done [14.10].

In November Annie, Catherine's sister, arrived for a visit, and Catherine remarked, 'Bert in his usual temper—Annie think him very cross'. November was a bad month for caterpillars and grasshoppers, and Catherine thought that Brandie Braes had more than its share. In December the first cricket team was formed in Lardner, and before

Christmas a party was planned for the children. Catherine recorded that 'Mr. Stoving gave money for tables and magic lantern. He is a *Brick*'. George Stoving was to present Catherine with a last chance for the life she craved.

1889

At the beginning of 1889, Catherine received a present of two new screens. They were very pretty, but she had no place to put them. 'I do wish I had a nice front room', she said, but 'I begin to think sometimes that I never shall have a nice house'. The fact that she had never had the house she wanted, and that there was little singing in her life, seemed to symbolise for Catherine the drudgery of a life filled with hard work and no rewards. But in June the Curries were given the chance of a new house and a new start when Mr Stoving asked them to move into Yuulong as tenants.

George Stoving had come to Australia from Germany in 1880 as one of the pioneers of the continental branch of the wool trade. In 1882 he opened an office in Melbourne for Wenz and Company of Rheims.[64] He was wealthy and well travelled, and Catherine already liked him for his generosity and the fact that he was a gentleman. After initial meetings, Catherine noted that she liked Yuulong very much, and on 10 June the terms were settled.

> *Stoving willing to take offer of 10/– per acre for the grass land and same for cultivation after it is cleared and ploughed, Daa to keep the ferns out . . . Surely if anyone can make it pay we ought to. Oh I hope and trust we will.*

On 28 June Mr Stoving 'seemed glad to see us' when Catherine and John, Fern and Rose moved in.

Just the two wee lassies came tonight. They are surprised and pleased, have been racing up and down the large Dining room with the Boots off. Daa in the Lairds room taking his whiskey and for myself I seem to enjoy this time by myself.

Mr Stoving had become the 'laird' or the 'squire', and Catherine admitted to feeling 'pleased as well as a bit anxious' about the new arrangement. As usual she worried about John and noted on 1 July, 'I like it well. Daa will be a bit I think before he feels at Home'.

At first it seemed to Catherine that she had attained the position that was due to her. The neighbours were all surprised to hear the news, which the Curries had kept to themselves, and life changed when the squire came to Yuulong from his business in Melbourne: 'when the Squire is here our midday meal is Luncheon. We dine at 7 pm quite aristocratic' [7.7]. The Curries still worked as hard as ever, now coping with two farms, and building a dairy at Yuulong. But Catherine was pleased to be living in a finer house, and to see John employing men to work for him, even if these workmen could not be trusted to work as hard as they should.

Mr Stoving often brought his friends to stay, and Catherine cooked and cleaned for them. Mr Kreafft was one of the first visitors, and created a good impression by bringing Catherine a 'very pretty and useful needle case, just the very thing I needed'. Mr Kreafft visited again in August, and John took him to Brandie Braes, where he took 'all sort of plants' from the garden. In December, when Mr Stoving made his last visit of the year, he seemed 'pleased with everything'.

1890

The next year, 1890, began with fires, and the diary noted on 30 January, 'Fire at BB—all Daa could do to save the barn, the grass garden all burnt. Such a day'. Stockdale had fired his scrub, and the sawmill was burnt down. Five miles of fences were burnt, and Gregory's fences and sheds were destroyed. Mr Stoving and Mr Kreafft arrived in the middle of the drama, and received only scant notice in a diary full of tales of fire and the eventual fining of Stockdale for wilfully setting a fire. 'Grand rain' fell in February, and on 24 February a letter came from Mr Kreafft sending money for John's expenses to Melbourne. John was 'very cross about the paltry cheque', but set out for Melbourne on 26 February. In March he had returned and was having arguments with a carpenter, Catherine was disgusted at the price of butter, and in the middle of the month the fires started up again. Catherine had very bad headaches through April, and in May John was upset about fights with workmen. Bert was happy to give up his mail round in June, as Catherine had not applied to renew the contract, but at the end of the financial year despair had set in again.

1.7   *This starts another year. Oh I pray that it may be better than last year. Daa has almost lost hope and no wonder.*

A few days later Catherine noted that the wallabies were 'making havoc'.

The stress was beginning to tell on John, and in August Catherine recorded a bad day. Mr Kreafft had interfered with John's orders to his least-favoured workman, Tromph, and John became angry and told them both some 'Home Truths'.

4.8   *. . . I think he frightened Mr K Perhaps Mr T too—but oh Dear I feel dreadful upset, I do wish John would not get cross with the workmen. at any rate he certainly should not have talked to Kreafft as he did. And Tromph there. I can't help feeling as if I was liveing in a powder mine, that might blow up any minute.*

All was not well between Catherine and John.

8.9   *This is the twenty-sixth anniversary of our wedding. It seems a very short time sometimes, we have had a lot of trouble and I can't hope now that things will be better. I think it is the Strikes that is Darkening the Horizon at present.*

Later that month John was cross with Catherine's friend Mrs Cornish, and Catherine noted, 'Mrs Cornish is quite broken hearted about Currie being cross'. It seems that the responsibility of managing another man's property was already beginning to tell on John, and in October Catherine thought it was unfair that he should take his temper out on her.

14.10   *I am oh so unhappy—Daa got cross for no reason at all this morning—I only said I had no place to set a Hen and he just oh what shall I do but think he never cared for me at all. Has it been all a mistake together I am sure I always try to Do for the best but I don't feel like trying any more today.*

The feeling of being among the 'aristocracy' was also wearing thin, and when Mr Kreafft wrote ordering the trap, Catherine remarked, 'such a way to write to us. Just the same as tho we were their Paid Servants'.

1891

Catherine was still striving rather desperately to give her children a better life than her own. In February 1891 she took Fern and Rose for a drive to Drouin.

24.2   *Daa would not let me take them so we did not ask today. They were delighted poor little things. I begin to think if they do not have pleasures in childhood they are not likely to have any in womanhood. Woman has so few. Better grasp them in passing.*

In July Auntie Jane Cunningham came to visit for the first time in five years. In September Catherine was complaining of her sons, who had not come to collect her when it was raining, but in November she added another boy to her family when she took in Harry, a boy from the Home for Destitute Children. He was supposed to work for his keep, but Catherine discovered that he did not have his certificate, and therefore would have to go to school. Her old generosity surfaced again, and she decided that she was not sorry that he should go to school and be treated 'as one of my own'.

In December Catherine was accosted by a tramp on the track, and fought him off with her whip. This was one of the few incidents to remind her of the depression. Her own personal depression was much more real to her.

1892

In March 1892 a bull broke out and John was in 'a great rage'.

26.3   *Oh dear I do wish he would not get into these unreasonable tempers. He allways make me quite ill but he never knows it, only says it is* my fault all the time.

Mr Kreafft was also annoying Catherine.

6.8   *I don't think he has a very good opinion of working folks in General and I know he never misses a chance of taking himself all he can get and it never lowers him in his own estimation and of course he measures other peoples corn by his own measure. Bother things.*

Mr Stoving was still one of her favourite people, and always came with presents from his overseas trips. In October he and his colleague Mr Wenz came to bring Catherine a boa from Aden and lace from Malta for Katie.

    Perhaps the worst development for Catherine was the deterioration of her relationship with all her children. She had always had fights with Bert, but now it was her favourite son Tom who provoked her.

1.12   *Tom tells me today that I always look at the worst side of people. I think he must be mistaken as I told him as I find people when I know them better to be not so good as I thought they were, even my own son Tom—will he ever know how much he hurt me when he said so. If I begin to write like this I must keep my book out of sight but it is hard to always pretend you don't care—none of my children will ever know their mother.*

1893

February 1893 was the usual month of fires, and in March Catherine was insulted by Bert. 'I am not well', Catherine said, 'tho I pretend I am and things hurt me'. In April the diary recorded that the Commercial Bank had closed its doors; a few days later the ES&A

followed suit, and in May it was the National. In August Harry was sent back to the home.

The drama of the bank failures was given only a line in the diary. Many people in rural areas would have been damaged by this disaster, although it appears that the Curries may not have been affected in any major way. In any case, Catherine was more concerned in the diary with her own health than with the health of the national economy. She suffered constant headaches and bouts of giddiness, and near the end of the year was still complaining about her children.

16.12   *I fell out with both my sons today. There is something in the air of Australia I think that prevents Boys having any respect for their parents. Of course I hear the Aborigines always put the old folk out of the way when they grow old.*

The next day she had a headache, because 'I was so upset yesterday'.

Hierarchies

A family tree, like a giant mountain ash, has firm roots in the soil, with branches spreading vertically and horizontally. A community, like a forest, is composed of family trees, intermingling. Some family trees grow taller than others, survive the bushfires and the disappointments of life, increasing in wealth and standing. Sometimes branches are stunted or cut off, sometimes whole families disappear. Natural selection is about successful ancestors; about members of the species who have proved themselves capable of propagating and reproducing little saplings in their own image. Human selection is a little more complicated than that.

By 1936, sixty years had passed since the first settlement at Lardner. Sixty years represented two generations of white inhabitants, and now there were names on headstones to mark the territory, and the ghosts were no longer absent. On New Year's Day in 1936 about six hundred people, past and present residents of Lardner, met at a 'Back to Lardner' gathering. At half-past eleven there was a roll-call of former scholars in the schoolyard, and they all went in to take their seats with much jocularity. Tom Currie and Ewan McPherson were oldest among the former boy scholars, Katie Currie and Annie McPherson the oldest remaining girl pupils. After 'school' there was a picnic lunch

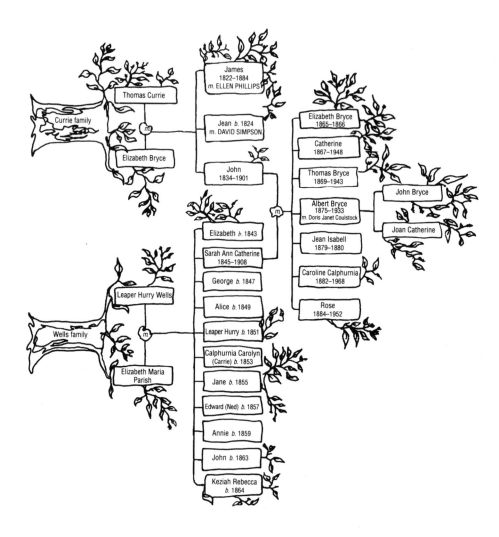

The Wells and Currie family trees, showing the branches connecting Catherine and John. *Drawn by Sally Esse.*

under the trees, and then Tom Currie gave an address, recalling that he had arrived at Lardner in 1875 when he was six years of age. He remembered being very frightened of the 'bears' and dingoes in the bush, but his earliest recollection was of the first picnic, held on Mr Hankey's property in November 1876, when Mr McPherson played the bagpipes. After Tom's speech, there were foot races, highland dancing, and a cricket match between past and present residents. There was much reminiscing about pioneering days, and the reunion ended with a grand 'comeback' ball in the evening. Although most of the 'comebacks' had left many years before, they retained 'a soft spot in their hearts for Lardner'.[65]

The surviving members of the Currie and McPherson families were the elite at this gathering held to celebrate European settlement in the Lardner district. They were the children of the first settlers, and had been part of the community from its beginning. They had grown into fine, hardworking citizens of good Scottish stock who could recall the hardships of the early life, but who now remembered, more strongly than the fear and the sacrifice, the good times and the friendships of the pioneering days. The old man who stood up to speak at the celebration had been weathered by the Gippsland sun and rain, gnarled by the ancient trees he had chopped down, and toughened by the hardships of his outdoor life. But he stood proudly as a member of one of the first Lardner families, and as a symbol and survivor of this community which the Curries had helped to create with the work of their own hands.

Most of those who were at this gathering had been born in Australia. Many of them had lived in Gippsland all their lives, and had been shaped by the family and community, the mental and physical landscape that had surrounded them since birth. This was the legacy which they shared, this 'soft spot in their hearts for Lardner'. Yet most of them had parents who had been born in another place, and the legacy of parents was also part of the surroundings that had shaped them. In many cases, this was also a joint inheritance.

Members of the Currie family knew their history well. In 1854 twenty-year-old shepherd John Currie had left his home near Edinburgh to travel to the goldfields of Australia. John had been born on 11 June 1834 to Thomas and Elizabeth Currie (formerly Bryce) in the Midlothian town of West Calder in Scotland. The village was located on a cold peat moor nearly five hundred feet above sea level; it had grown up on the route between Edinburgh and Glasgow and by 1841 had a population of under two thousand people. Much of the land was not worth cultivating as it was exposed to wind and rain from the south and south-west, but it enjoyed fine distant views to the north over lower country. Perhaps it was this which later encouraged the Curries to build every house they owned on a hill.

In his history of West Calder, W. C. Learmonth says:

> In almost every instance the local situations of men form their characters. The inhabitants of this parish are much excluded from the commerce of the world, and nearly all on a level with regard to each other. Their attention is directed to few objects, and hence they are simple and unaffected in their manners; while they possess a wonderful degree of sagacity in and acuteness in everything connected with their circle of pursuits. From the great number of poor farms, every individual may look forward to an establishment in life; and hence his attention to business and industry is excited. In this state of society, it must be confessed, there is little scope for ambition which impels a man to rise above his humble sphere; but this situation supposes contentment and happiness.[66]

West Calder was a religious place, where 'drunkenness and debauchery of all sorts are scarcely known'.[67] Living in the same district were families with names that would surround John for the rest of his life, first at Ballan and later at Lardner—McKays, Hamiltons, Greenshields, Cunninghams, Hardies and Blacks. These were people who were not sufficiently filled with 'contentment and happiness' to remain on their poor farms in West Calder. They transplanted many of their ambitions and beliefs to their new land, and it was these that decided the characteristics of the local community they formed at Lardner.

In an article on New Zealand pioneering communities in the nineteenth century, Miles Fairbairn reviews the theme that New Zealand society was a combination of many insulated and uniform local communities. The theme has been developed by several New Zealand historians, including W. H. Oliver:

> The pioneering experience was centrifugal in a geographical way—that is, it separated people into more rather than less distinct locational groupings. But socially and within each locality it was centripetal in its effect; it drew individuals into the vortex of the locality, and within that vortex social differences were not so much obliterated as enveloped.[68]

This lack of division and tension, Oliver suggests, was further fostered by the similar experiences of settlers and their membership of the same institutions: church, lodge, cricket team or school.

In testing this model, Fairbairn suggests that we should examine three possible types of social bonding: 'We shall call these categories of association the kinship, the vertical and the horizontal'.[69] Fairbairn's examination extends much wider than one community and the evidence of one diary, but his three categories are useful guides in a more specific examination of the Currie family and its local community. Within these three categories of association were subtle divisions of power and wealth, and these were embodied within the structures of family and community that people inherited or created.

The basic tie was that of kinship, and on Lardner's Track the basic unit was the nuclear family. Most settlers were couples with young children; indeed many, like John Currie, moved to Lardner in the hope of obtaining enough land to support their growing families. These families conformed to the traditional view that the man was the head of the household and had the final word; the man was the bread-winner, the wife the keeper of home and family. This division may not have manifested itself in roles that were as clear cut as those of city families, for in the country the wife was constantly present at the work place, and was called upon to assist with even the heavy tasks when an extra hand was required. Catherine did her own traditional jobs of milking, butter-making, cooking and cleaning, but she also worked beside John in field and garden. The children too contributed their labour to the farm, regardless of sex and age. Yet John was still the final arbiter on matters affecting farm and family.

It seems, at least from Catherine's record of events, that in many ways she was the dominant personality. John was self-contained and solitary, and often disappeared into the paddocks when visitors called, leaving Catherine to dispense the social niceties along with the produce of her garden. Yet on certain matters regarding the running of the farm he was adamant, and no matter how desperately Catherine pleaded with him to delay a burn, he was determined that it should be his decision. When neighbours came to discuss serious political or social matters, it was John's advice they sought.

If Catherine found this galling, she did not openly express discontent. Whatever complaints may have been privately confided to her diary, the family presented a united front to the world, all members publicly conforming to the roles demanded of them. The sons were taken out to be trained by their father in the work of the farm, and an axe was placed in their hands as soon as they were strong enough to swing it. The girls helped with the milking and the butter-making and some of the harder labouring work, but there was no glamour attached to this women's work, unlike the praise given to the boy who demonstrated his growing masculine strength. As they grew older, girls were encased in the tight corsets and stiff, starched petticoats that would necessarily preclude any unseemly or unfeminine activity.

The hierarchy of the family extended from the husband to the wife, and then down to the small children. Catherine was proud of her children, and she loved them, but she was determined that they should be brought up to respect their parents and other adults. Discipline was handed out with something that looks to the modern reader like ferocity; Fern was whipped for a misdemeanour before she was a year old. Such strict measures were not uncommon when applied to small children, but it seems that Catherine did not know when to stop. She fought hard to maintain her dominance over her children, even when they became too old to be spanked and she had to devise other punishments. Bert was twenty-two years old when she threw a bucket of water over him one cold morning when he had slept in. It was obvious to everyone but the mother that such tactics would only lose her the respect, and possibly the love, of her children, and as the family grew older the relationship deteriorated.

Kinship ties extended also to the wider family, and often the attempt to establish hierarchical ties here also brought conflict. According to Fairbairn's model, there would need to be strong family loyalties, extended families in the same area, and a high rate of intermarriage if the kinship mode was to be significant. Lardner did have extended families, and many of these already had links through marriages which had taken place at Ballan. Fairbairn does not say whether the extended family needed to live harmoniously in order to constitute strong kinship loyalties. While an extended family provided support, it also occasionally proved a burden. By the time of the move to Lardner, James Currie was a sick and broken widower with failing eyesight and memory. In the diary, Catherine often complained about the extra work he gave both herself and John. It seems that James did not appreciate their 'care', and sometimes swore at Catherine.

As families moved together into Gippsland, they brought with them those old or ill relatives who could not be left behind bereft of family support. Often such extended families moved into the new territory together for reasons of pragmatism as well as sentiment. John brought his ailing brother James in order to look after him, but also to use his name in selecting land. Similarly, the Hardies brought Mrs Hardie's sister, Elizabeth Broad, to select and settle on the property beside them. In fact most of the Hardie family lived at Elizabeth's Broadwood, for she was too ill to manage it herself. As a single woman, it is unlikely that she would have run the property on her own, even if she had been in the best of health. When she died of cancer, her land was left to the Hardie family.

The family and the extended family provided essential support. Catherine had cared for her younger sister Jane since the death of her mother, and soon after the Curries moved to Gippsland, Jane married Cornelius (Neil) Cunningham, who selected a block of land just down the track from the Currie property. At first there was constant visiting, with John and Neil helping each other with clearing and planting, and exchanging implements and horses. Jane depended on Catherine and the older Currie children for help with her babies and her house. But friction arose when Neil refused to be sufficiently grateful for Catherine's help and advice, and eventually the families parted in acrimony.

The Curries had moved away from the Wells family, who had been close by at Ballan, but they were visited at Lardner by most members of the family. Older sister Lizzie, who was seen as the surrogate mother, was expected to arrive in time to take over the house and family when Catherine or Jane were confined with new babies, or at times of disaster or illness. Ned and John arrived sometimes to help on the farm, often to some complaining from Catherine that they were under-worked and overpaid. Leaper, the brother in Melbourne, came with his wife to visit occasionally, and was of some assistance when Catherine was taken to the Melbourne asylum. Sister Carrie came to visit immediately after she was married, bringing her new husband to meet the Curries.

Within the family there were subtle links of power, unspoken hier-archies. The old and ill were at the mercy of the fit, for the family was the only refuge for those no longer able to earn a living. The woman gained her status as the preserver of cultural and social values, and saw her worth reflected in the good manners and clean clothes of her children. But the family was dependent on the strength of the husband and father, and it was the hardest-working and strongest man who would clear his land most quickly, produce strong sons to help him farm the land, and so reap bigger crops and monetary rewards. Eventually he would be able to build a bigger house, maybe import a piano from England, and bring more singing and status into the lives of his wife and children. The measure of a man was therefore em-bedded in the notion of the work ethic, for in this seemingly egali-tarian society, work—hard physical work—would earn more respect than any other achievement. When Tom Currie stood up to speak at the 1936 Lardner reunion he was a hero not only because he was a surviving pioneer, but because of his reputation as an axeman. It was generally agreed in the district that both Bert and Katie knew more about farming, but Tom had been able to fell a tree faster and better than any other man.

At the beginning, though, all the settlers appeared to be roughly equal in wealth and status. In a community of selectors, each with roughly the same quantity and quality of land, each with the same resources and problems, it seemed that the promise of an egalitarian society would be fulfilled. Add to this the Australasian ethic of mateship and equality, and the community would be formed on the basis of a democratic and equal society. Fairbairn's second model, of vertical bonding, is of relationships 'in which power is unevenly distributed and the powerful exact obedience and compliance from the weak'.[70] Such relationships did not seem to be strongly present in New Zealand, for similar reasons that they were absent in the Lardner community, and Fairbairn posits the idea of more subtle vertical hierarchies than those of class or power:

> The juxtaposition of these curbs on social power and opportunities for material independence had the effect of imbedding the work ethic in the notion of good character while depreciating the value placed on obedience to constituted authority. They also set up a selective egalitarianism: it was the individual's destiny to be his own boss but not to boss other people about. By implication, acquiring wealth was more acceptable than dominating other people.[71]

Fairbairn suggests that the unequal vertical relationships in the colonies were built on less elitist and ingrained social bonds than those that existed in the old world. The Gippsland community did not rely on personal power, but on success and material possessions:

> Material possessions, especially the roomy house, were a much more effective medium for advertising superior social status than the invisible threads of personal power. But what was pivotal to the separation of wealth from power was that the conditions of material life multiplied the numbers of the self-employed and petty proprietors at the expense of large employers.[72]

The major ties in this community were those which Fairbairn has characterised as horizontal: associations between people who were roughly equal in wealth and social standing. The horizontal bonding mechanisms were generated by the dense framework of networks and groups, and were the result of frequent collaboration and interaction. There were always, of course, some subtle differences.

As in any 'horizontal' community, there were always some who were more equal than others. Catherine Currie would accept the well-educated Hardies as equals, but her diary made it clear what she thought of the hard-drinking Symes. Yet this is not to deny her generosity, and her community spirit. She wrote letters for the illiterate Walter McKay and visited with her doctor's book when any of the neighbours were sick. When Mr Stevens fathered an illegitimate child there was much scandal and gossip in the district, but Catherine confided no harsh judgements in her diary, only noting that she felt sorry for the two women involved and the 'poor little baby'. Sometimes this non-judgemental approach took forms which appeared almost bizarre. When Syme killed poor old Walter McKay, a close friend and neighbour, the Curries soon accepted Syme back as a visitor to their house.

From the beginning Lardner was a close-knit community, where forgiveness of others' idiosyncrasies, or even crimes, was necessary for harmonious living. People made an effort to visit each other, for exchanges of pleasant conversation, manual labour or vital farming implements. In the bush, rough bark huts were built in tiny clearings that gradually grew larger as the axemen chipped away at the edges of the forest. By Australian standards the huts were not great distances from each other, but they were obscured from sight by the trees, and the tracks between them were rapidly overgrown or blocked by fallen logs. It took hard work to keep them open, so that people could pass from house to house. In winter, some of the tracks were impassable after rain, and too dangerous to negotiate at night. In spite of these problems, there was constant passage from hut to hut. Catherine's diary records at least one visitor nearly every day, and often there were several. Not all were friends; strangers arrived seeking information or shelter, and the lore of the bush demanded that such people were treated with courtesy and consideration. Most of this human interaction devolved on the woman of the house, who was usually closer to house and garden than the man who spent his daylight hours felling trees or ploughing paddocks.

The informal community relationships were soon given institutional form. The beginnings of the community at Lardner in the 1870s were not arbitrary or haphazard. There was a framework to build on and an order to be followed, and those people who had already worked together at Ballan knew from instinct and practice how a good community should be run. Just as there were certain unwritten neighbourly rights and obligations, so there were institutions to set up and support, institutions that would strengthen and safeguard the rights and duties of the members of the community. As huts were built and gardens planted, tracks cut and trees felled, plans were hastily made for the establishment of a school and a church. Civilisation was not only about using the land productively and for material gain; it was also about the finer things of life, such as learning and faith, and passing on traditions to the next generation.

As early as 1876, the settlers of Lardner's Track were writing to the Education Department to ask that a school be built in the area. Inspector Holland came by coach on a visit of enquiry, and within a few weeks the first teacher had arrived. The school began in the slab hut belonging to Lachlan Grant, and Thomas Collingwood was the first teacher. The same building was used for the first Presbyterian church service, held by the Reverend Morton of Dandenong. A site was reserved for a more permanent school building, and in 1877 a portable school was brought from Melbourne and erected on this block.[73]

While small temporary buildings were used for the first meetings, school and church, it was important for the community to have a building that could serve as a permanent meeting place for conversation or complaint, for dances or debates, for singing or sermons or socials. The saga of the Mechanics Hall was a fine example of the community at work; of collaboration marred by conflict, of the difficulties encountered in a community of proudly self-reliant individuals who were very dependent on one another. This was a community isolated by distance and life-style from the softer people of the cities, and although proximity sometimes led to conflict, these people understood each other, for they shared the same aspirations and values, many of them inculcated in childhoods spent in West Calder.

The horizontal bonds that linked people roughly equal in power were the primary ties between the families of the community. And yet within these relationships there were petty squabbles and grimmer conflicts that went to establish a pecking order and a hierarchy based on respectability, literacy and decency. In New Zealand, says Fairbairn, it is 'inconceivable that the *local community* was organized on the basis of client/patron relationships.'[74] And yet in the Lardner community, there was still a subtle structuring of people into vertical positions.

There were some relationships that showed very clearly that the old world classifications of class and wealth were not entirely moribund in Australia, not even in such a homogeneous community as Lardner. It is the Curries' relationship with George Stoving that illustrates this most clearly. Stoving was the rich outsider, a foreigner, and therefore a trifle exotic. He was also a 'civilised' man, and a true gentleman. He was a patron of the community, buying books for the Mechanics Institute, helping with the children's parties, and making donations to all the community efforts and causes. He did not participate in the local contest to find the best worker, for he himself did no physical work. But he was polite and good-mannered, deferring to John for advice about the farm and, apart from bringing gifts for Catherine and the girls when he returned from overseas, making no great display of his superior wealth and position.

In her diary, Catherine referred to Stoving as 'the laird' and 'the squire', and although her references were self-mocking, they contained an edge of true deference. Stoving offered Catherine a chance to taste the good life, to live in a big house and see her husband managing other men and drinking whisky with the squire in his study. For all the lip-service to egalitarian colonial ways, the vertical bonds were still present.

There was always a conflict here. While Catherine was happy to work for a gentleman, and perhaps therefore rise above her neighbours by the old world route, she did not like to do tasks usually reserved for servants, such as collecting visitors from the station. In Lardner, where the ideal was the family farm which used family labour, people avoided using wage labour, and when extra work was needed it was usually done by other farmers working on contract, just as John worked for Stoving. John's personality and background had not prepared him to be an employer. In West Calder, wage labour could not be afforded, and John had little experience and was not comfortable when in charge of hired men. Both he and Catherine appeared to expect their hired hands to demonstrate the same level of commitment to the property as they themselves showed, and they became frustrated and angry when this was not forthcoming.

The commitment of the self-employed, the proprietor farmer, could not be denied. Within two generations, the white settlers had changed the landscape at Lardner. Their hard work had changed the forest into pastures, and their children would reap the benefits of a landscape that now was no longer at the edge of the world. Within two generations the mental landscape had also been irrevocably changed.

By 1936 the world had been through one world war, and only vaguely guessed that it would soon be embroiled in another. As the 'comebacks' celebrated their return to Lardner, they were celebrating simpler days, a time when the community was smaller and more self-contained, when the horizontal and vertical bonds were more clear cut. Now the community contained the notion of the Anzacs, a different knowledge of the world and its hierarchies of value and heroism.

A family tree, like a mountain ash, has firm roots in the soil from which it grows. From the peat moor of West Calder and the town of Ipswich, to the forest of Lardner, the Currie family tree drew its nutrients and carried its inheritance. A community, like a forest, is composed of family trees, intermingling. But human selection is not only about survival of the fittest, but about the way people fit into their own, manufactured landscapes. Sociologist Peter Berger has suggested that every individual biography is an episode within the history of society. In every life there is an inner myth, a personal and psychological dimension, and a manifest myth, which is constructed by historical and social conditions. Berger describes this as a 'sacred canopy', and in describing it, James Veninger has said:

> The human community, in its pursuit of order and meaning, creates necessary structures, an objective world of ideas and values that, after a time, comes to confront the individual as a powerful reality separated from its human origins. Order in a society is preserved as long as this objective reality is affirmed by the individual ... Berger has an apt metaphor for the objective reality that man creates: the sacred canopy ... The fate and freedom that we learn about through biography have as their foundation the sacred canopies of a given time and place.[75]

The objective reality that a society creates exists in institutions, in values and in language. When Catherine Currie began her diary, she was securely situated beneath the sacred canopy, and she understood its limits and its demands. But at some point, boundaries were crossed, and she moved out from beneath the umbrella which gave shelter to all sane and civilised beings. Catherine crossed the boundary and gained her knowledge of transgression.

It is perhaps unfortunate for Catherine that this experience is what has made her interesting. Darryl Reanney has described the medium of language as 'the mode of heredity outside the genes',[76] and it is through her account of dislocation and discontinuity that Catherine has selected herself as part of our modern history. She had undertaken a heroic enterprise; living on the boundary between the written and the unwritten, she managed to fill the silence with her words. But the story did not fulfil her expectations, for somewhere she had expected that her narrative would give her a share of human happiness.

Happiness has sometimes been a promise of the narrative, but it has never been a promise of the grand theory of evolution. Survival, this theory says, is enough. In 1936, as the children of the pioneers gathered to celebrate their survival, they had their own well-known ghosts to haunt the land. Familiar names were inscribed on the headstones around the church, the experience of their ancestors could be read in the words that had survived in diaries and letters. This tangible presence of ancestors was something which the first pioneers had always mourned and lacked, and now the community celebrated the presence of a generation which relieved the loneliness for those who came after them.

Catherine's diary, like her life, was now part of the archaeology, one of the lateral layers of history. As Tom stood up to address the 1936 meeting, he was part of the evidence that she had been successful in passing on her genes to the next generation. In a biological sense, her life had been sufficient. The family tree still grew, although it was now slightly stunted; Catherine's five surviving children would produce only two children for the next generation.* Her survival was of a different order, for her mode of heredity existed in language.

It is often difficult to find the place or the time where one sacred canopy is replaced by another. Berger says that 'in periods of great social, cultural and political turmoil, individuals doubt the truth to this objective reality, and such alienation gives way to new ideas and new values'.[77] But it is hard to find a boundary between sacred canopies. By 1936 Catherine had been given a different place in the hierarchy from the one she had occupied in life. Today her story carries a different weight and meaning beneath a slightly less than sacred canopy. The story remains the same, the words endure between the covers of the diary. But removed from the shelter of Catherine's sacred canopy, the meaning of the words and the way we interpret them has been changed. History has given them a different place in the hierarchy.

---

* Bert married after his mother's death, and had two children. None of the other children married.

Endings 1894–1908

1894

By 1894 the diary Catherine was keeping was very different from the one she had started twenty years before. The writing was less neat, and the entries now longer and more personal. Her book had become more a confessional than a record of a farming life; it still recorded John's work, but the emphasis now was on Catherine's experience. And a sorry one it was.

1.1.94   *Monday very fine Day indeed. Katie did her washing and Ironing. Daa and Bert mending fences and painting gates, all very busy. Have not made a good start. Daa scolding this morning and oh I am just so miserable why does he—I do not seem to have a Friend on earth. Not one cares if I am sorry or glad. If I had not a Heavenly father to go to I could not live at all—how do any one live that have not faith. That all things must work for our good even tho we will not see it in this world—I have been unhappy all my life, seem to have been one long struggle. No wonder I envy those that die, they are well if they die in the Lord. Perhaps I shall not live long. Then they will miss me a little. Very little.*

144

Other people were not having such a bad time, as she recorded in her next entry on John and the children.

2.1   *Very fine day the young folk at the Dance last night. They all enjoyed themselves very much. Bob W drove his sisters and Janet Kyle here. Katie did not go to bed, she says. She never felt as well after a Dance. Mr Stoving and Mr Keep came. Daa went to meet them at the station. Mr S looking very pleased and well, Mr Keep could not stay all night, they took him in the trap to Jackson Hill Bert took Dimple and Wallace to take home Jem Wilkinsons machine. I hope he got there safe but am very anxious about him, but as usual I pretend I am not. All pretence.*

By 4 January John had been forgiven for his scolding. Catherine was pleased to see him 'killing time' with Mr Stoving for 'how can he help getting cross when he works harder than he is able'. But on the same day Bert gave her cheek when she asked him to drive Katie to Drouin with the butter.

Why do I let him vex me, but I am only like dirt under all their feet. Why should Katie go and let Bert loaf about. I fly round to attend to the rest, I am not really able but I pretend I am, and they don't know any better but I do get so tired, and it seems Lazy to lie down—but I have to some times, I hear them asking where's Mother—Rosie says lieing down somewhere. See I get credit for lieing down oftener than I do. I must lock up my Book, or I must not write so much. Bert took the butter.

In spite of her tiredness and weakness, the diary made it clear that she was still dominating her family.

On 13 January Catherine was still trying to keep the upper hand, this time with her neighbour Mrs McFarlane. Catherine had been making a tie for Tom, more meticulously than such a task would seem to warrant.

Mrs McFarlane told me I was not doing it right, before she even saw it. When she did it was quite right but I was not pleased then, neither was she as she knew she had spoken too quick, but Jeannie Hardie says that it is just her way, they can do nothing right but she has allways a pick at me since I once had a game of Draughts with her. I won it, I had not played for more than a Dozen years, told her so before starting. She had played every evening, her husband is or was a Don at it, it was quite as much to my surprise as hers that I won but it was a long game. She seemed to study it well. Mrs Hardie congratulated me on winning, but Mrs Mac has never forgiven me, poor body. She has had a lot of Trouble since I saw her last. I would like to be nice to her for she has lost both her Daughter and her Husband since those days but she must try to patronise me, and I don't like it.

Three days later, the real problem surfaced.

16.1.94 *Very Severe Frost last night, seems strange Harvest weather. Daa went to Council Meeting to Day left the Boys to reap. They are good Boys but they care no more for me than I do for the old pig. I am sure I think more of every other living thing than they do for me, they came in and Scolded about their Dinner not being ready, when it was the same as usual, but their Father not here, and it was not worth while to be civil to their mother—oh I am so disappointed in my children. I thought they could not help loving their Mother, but I have never had their respect since their Father shut me up in a Lunatic Assylum. That was a Dreadful misfortune but it was not his fault as he only did as he was advised by the Stupid people I had here. I remember it all so well so well that morning. They took me away Saturday Morning 17 Sep 1881. I only begged to be put in a nice clean bed, I was better if they could have seen it. I had been ill, they nursed me (two nights) then took me off to a Lunatic Assylum tied up in an old corn sack, is it any wonder that I raved. Oh I shall write it all some day when I have time. I have always intended to, I am always thinking of it when they vex me. I always put it all down to that, or I could have won their respect.*

Writing this out seemed to have taken some of the load off Catherine's mind, for the months proceeded with only brief complaints of Bert 'blaming me as usual', when he came in hot and tired after reaping [25.1].

In March Bert was still causing trouble, and on 16 March Catherine complained, 'Bert was three hours away at the post . . . I must thrash him next time he is long it looks bad to see boys idling'. The diary became a trifle disorganised as Catherine skipped a few pages by mistake and April entries appeared in the middle of February. On 5 April Catherine was 'very anxious somehow', and on 15 April she recorded, 'I am very anxious these times'. Sometimes the writing became hard to read as Catherine complained of feeling 'shaky', but she usually recorded feeling better the next day, and went back to work.

In May Catherine recorded for the first time the anniversary of the death of her first baby, Elizabeth, who had died at Ballan before the move to Lardner.

29.5.94   *Today is our eldest Daughter's Birthday. She died Bless her just one week before she saw the Anniversary, also Leps my Brothers.*

On 4 July Catherine was ill, and the next day Mr Learoyd and Mr Kreafft arrived.

4.6   *... I am not well, oh Dear how can I do all I have to Do can I never get a rest. I did not use to want a rest, but now I do not feel able to crawl, nobody minds.*

5.7   *... Daa went to Drouin to meet Mr Learoyd and Kreafft, I think it was the thought of him coming made me feel so ill yesterday. He is here now Bother him. I don't like him, he forgets that it is not his wife that has to clear after him*

6.7   *... Mr Learoyd told us he is going to join the noble army of Benedicts, I wish him every Happiness. He is a Dear he deserve to be Happy.*

It is difficult to know what this entry signified, as a newspaper cutting announcing Mr Learoyd's marriage is inserted at the front of this volume of the diary.

Catherine was obviously becoming more unreasonable, and John did not seem to remember his old promises and resolutions of 1881. His patience was wearing thin.

15.8   *Cold showers to Day. Daa just finished his ploughing for oats this morning, Bert thought to finish yesterday, left early to go to John Hardies Funeral Bert and Daa, I cannot write but oh what is the use of living. Daa got oh so cross, he said to Tom are you coming, Tom says no. Mother thinks we need not all go, then the storm began. I had said nothing to Tom since last night, but to Daa this morning that I thought they need not all go, he said he ought to go, that I thought I was right, what did he mean by Flaring up when Tom said Mother thinks we need not all go, I can't see yet why they all should go, but Daa said all sorts of hard things. I was the most unreasonable woman that ever was. Perhaps I have not been right this while but I have not been well. This should excuse.*

On 10 September Tom set off for the goldfields of Western Australia, but soon wrote to say he was coming home again in November.

2.11   *. . . letter from Tom, Dear old chap says he is coming home, am so glad we all are, Daa even more than I, am much afraid he has not been well, oh Dear such a place to be ill in, cannot get a wash even. Shall weary till I see him now. I expect he is just Skin and bone— have never felt so anxious yet as now, as I fear he is very unwell, he is not used to roughing it, it must be very unhealthy tinned food all the time, and so little water. I do wish he was home.*

Like a self-fulfilling prophesy Tom returned on 9 November, 'looking very thin and brown, quite 5 years older than when he left for Coolgardie'. Tom himself claimed that he had 'had no hardship'.

Tom was following the family tradition of both his maternal and paternal ancestors, heading off as the Curries and the Wells had done for the latest gold rush. The dream of wealth which had lured his parents to the land had turned sour, and the Depression seemed to be negating much of the hard work the family had put in. There were no illusions now that those who worked hard would be suitably rewarded.

1895

January and February 1895 were hot and windy. Catherine anxiously noted the east wind, and on 13 February recorded 'the old old

February cry for rain'. On 17 February Catherine felt 'so frightened all the time', and that afternoon the fire came through.

> *The wind was coming fair north and just at the time the fire was coming strongest out the green trees—it came from the south for half an hour I think in answer to our prayers. So that we managed to save the place . . . we sat up till after 3 o'clock, AM, then the very welcome rain.*

The next day Catherine gave credit to the Lord and the Curries, and assigned blame.

> *I know it was the* Good Lord *watching us and we did what we could ourselves with His help—we think it must have been Jack Walsh that lit it. Was very wicked, for I wished him to be burned in it, but God will punish him in his own way. I feel it so, only he will not know why.*

The Good Lord was becoming a much more active protagonist in Catherine's diary, as her human actors disappointed her more and more. On 25 February Catherine had her fiftieth birthday, and mortality was much on her mind.

> 8.3.95 *. . . I asked Tom this morn. to grub a little stump in the garden. I was hurt and surprised when he said quite pleasantly no I won't, so I did it myself, what did it matter. Half an hour's very hard work for me and 6 blisters on my hands, when he could have done it in 3 minutes, this is the colonial respect for parents. How will he take it should he read this when I am no more.*

Three days later a new man arrived to work for Tom. Catherine complained that she 'knew nothing of it'.

> *This shows Boys think nothing of me—only for the work I can Do.*
> *I am not well. Nasty pain Back of my Head.*

On 19 March the income tax forms arrived, and Catherine complained 'oh Dear, I wish we had an income to pay the tax on. We would not mind the work, but we can't make it pay'. In April Tom was out fossicking for gold, but when John went to see the hole he had dug he could not see any gold: 'oh dear I wish we had some', said Catherine dolefully. Good Friday fell on 12 April, but everyone kept working, as they would rather be busy than 'loaf around'. In May Mr Stoving told Catherine that in future he would pay her board when he came to stay—three shillings a day for himself and his friends. Catherine thought 'Mr Currie' may not like it, so Stoving advised her not to tell him. Catherine gloated in private.

9.5   *... three shillings each a Day from the Day they come to the Day*
they leave both Days inclusive. Will be nice for me. I wonder what
Daa will say when I tell him.

When Mr Stoving left on 31 May he promised to send Catherine a cheque for £6 3s. 'I want it very much', Catherine confided to her diary. But like so many secret hopes, this one also was dashed. On 3 June a cheque for £25 arrived from Mr Stoving to pay John £20 he was owed, with £5 for Catherine on account. Catherine wailed:

> *I wish he had sent it direct to me. I get so little for anything and*
> *Daa gets so little that I do not like to ask him. Oh oh Dear, will*
> *things ever come right.*

George Stoving was obviously a man of good will and good manners, who did not fully understand the tensions of the household. He came from a different world, and his letters to the Curries came on the letterhead of the Menzies Hotel or the Tasmanian Club. But he shared a genuine bond with the Curries, for he was interested in all aspects of agriculture and horticulture, and relied on his manager for advice. John was something of an expert on sheep, and Stoving shared his passion for breeding. Letters preserved in the diary give an example of his interests and his concern for the Currie family and the farm, such as one written from the Tasmanian Club in Hobart on 24 March 1895. Addressed to Mr John Currie of Yuulong, it said:

> *Dear Sir,*
>
> *I received your last note announcing the wellcome rainfall and am so glad the troubles of fires are a thing of the past. I hope you got more rain than the 170 points—double the quantity would not have been too much.*
>
> *I wont be back for some time but then we will go through the sheep and I shall get a good expert to cull our studs. A very usefull thing I heard last week from one of our prominent breeders who saw that it would have been better if we had taken a Werringort ram also, instead of a Wool Wool and Merton park one, for the reason that the faringham flock was so poor and the sheep of such large frame that hardly any ram would fit as well as one of the new flock—in spite of the theory of inbreeding. We shall talk about it when I come up. Are we going to show some sheep at Melbourne this year or is it still too early—just think of that please. Give—a little more money for clearing on the road, we might as well have it done soon.*
>
> *I am glad our picket fence was not destroyed by the fire: I was very much afraid I suppose the contractor has not burnt his heaps in the road between Hardies and ourselves. Have you got a man to sink the hole in the swamp to see how deep the waterlevel lies, it would be well to have it done this autumn.*

> *I received your packet with the apples packed inside, I took*
> *them with me to Hobart, they are fine quality of fruit—I am*
> *living here in good style, plenty of friends and doing nothing—a*
> *real loaf with plenty of exercise.*
> *I hope you are all very well, my kind regards to everybody*
> *from yours very truly*
> *George Stoving.*

Stoving returned to Yuulong again in June, and began to teach
Rose and Fern to play golf. He corresponded often with the family, and
several of the letters are preserved in the diary. Occasionally, it seems,
the dates are wrong, and one letter dated July 1898 appears to have
been written in 1895. In a letter from the Menzies Hotel, Stoving
invited both Catherine and John to go to Melbourne to visit him. He
stressed particularly that Catherine was included in the invitation.

> *I want her v. much to come—see the sheep, the theater, my rooms*
> *—and the City—Mr Goold also—who is leaving for old Europe*
> *in perhaps 10 or 14 days—wishes to pass another evening with us*
> *for he enjoyed his stay at Yuulong and as I shall get you a nice room*
> *in a quiet Hotel—you had better make up your mind to come*
> *both—and send me a telegram so that I am ready and free for*
> *Monday morning at the time you are in town. Leave your travel-*
> *ling bag at the station, come up the Rialto straight from the train*
> *on Monday morning and you will have a 9 oclock breakfast in my*
> *rooms—which you will like—then we shall see the sheep—or see*
> *them in the afternoon and the Rialto Dairying company—some*
> *cream separators etc etc.*

The tone of the letter indicates that Stoving anticipated some
resistance to the idea of Catherine accompanying her husband to
Melbourne. In July the diary recorded that John had gone to

Melbourne, and Catherine noted that she was very disappointed not to go too. She wanted to see Mr Stoving's rooms in Melbourne.

Throughout this year Catherine had begun to add a little mantra at the end of many entries. After filling in an account of the work, the children's activities or arguments with John, she would add 'alls well'. All was not well. In July she suggested branding some sheep and John was cross. 'It is hard to be blamed when one thinks they ought to get credit rather', said Catherine. In August she was refusing to speak to Mrs McPherson, who had voted against John in the council election. In September she was still fighting with Bert: 'He is one of the sort that pretends to think his mother can do no good—only I try not to care and it seems that vexes him most' [4.9].

On 30 September Catherine recorded that she was preparing for 'our holiday trip tomorrow'. The next entry is dated three weeks later, and the thought and writing is rambling and confused.

20.10   *A very fine Day. We returned from our most eventful Trip last Monday. I am going to try and think Backwards for a while . . . such a time we had—we none of us will ever forget it, but I am home now, I do not regret going—but it is not as I expected it to be, simply because Mrs Johnstone would not let me do as I intended because of the expence. I feel just like swearing at her parsimony. I intended sleeping at Flack's Hotel and Breakfasting there, inviting them to Dine with me there then going to tea with my friends but they fairly drove me mad. With Dinning into my head that I could not afford it. We had a very pleasant time till we came to Grants then it seemed as tho it was all lies. I hate Lies. I could not sleep have not slept since I started to prepare for our trip. I know it is the worst thing that could be. Grant wished us to stay I think but he went the wrong way to work when he tried to force me, by saying he would take a switch to me if I did not behave.*

103 /8 /5

intended Sleeping at Ffd No Hotel
& breakfasting there, inviting them to dine with
me but then going to tea with my friends—
but they fairly drove me mad. Every Dunny
is to stay Dead, that I could not afford it
we had a very pleasant time, till
we came to Streets, then it seemed as tho
it was all lies. I hate Lies, I could
not Sleep, have not slept, & yca started
to Prepare for our trip, I know it is to
went Pretty Bad I can't by. Grant wished
us to stay & drink but he went the
wrong way to work, when he tried to
force me, by saying, he would take a
Switch to me if I did not behave I
suppose he thought I would take it as a joke
but he did not know how I had been just
Suffering, all my natural inclinations for
Years & Years. No one will ever know how I
suffered, & Pretended it was, just as I liked it,
when it was all Sammon. Just Sammon,
Fannie told me we must go, after I had
Paid for the Damage, as I came to the age the
children I thought I would do so they might
I had been looking for Dora, and they had
not sent my letters to him I think that
all Seemed to be against me, will write no
more now about it at this time, am home

From Catherine's diary, 20 October 1895

*Suppose he thought I would take it as a joke but he did not know
how I had been suppressing all my natural inclinations for years
and years. No one will ever know how I suffered, and pretended it
was just as I like it when it was all Gammon, just Gammon. Fernie
told me we must go, after I had paid for the Damage, as I came to
please the children I thought I would Do as they wished. I had been
looking for Daa and they had not sent my letters to him. I think
that all seemed to be against me. Will write no more now about it
at this time—am home.*

The following days the work of the farm went on, and Mrs Hardie
came to see Catherine with the news that Mrs Nottman, who had been
ill, was now recovered. 'I need not pity her', said Catherine, 'as they
would be all kind to her, where they are not always that to me, all
abuse me here right and left' [25.10]. The next day John came rushing in
to get a cheque, and 'nearly frightened my poor wits away again. I
think he might take time a little'. The entries went on, not always
coherent, although Catherine was obviously partly aware of what was
happening. When she went to visit a neighbour, 'all my Daughters
came to see me home. They are afraid to let me out of sight' [6.11]. She
was more and more obsessed with her children.

11.11 *I am not so well today perhaps only cross tho, those boys of mine
Do make we wild, I wonder what their private opinion of thier
mother is, they treat her just as tho she was here on Sufference. I am
very sure they will not miss me, a little bit, the ugliest girl and most
that could be gets more civility than I do from them. It makes me
feel as if oh I don't know but I am afraid to be near either of them
when their father is not here, and I am jealous of their smiles to
others. Fancy when Satan himself if their is such a one would not
make me afraid, it is only that I love them as never Mother loved
children I am very sure.*

The doctor called to see her, but this only upset her more.

13.11   *I went in evening to see Mrs Notman . . . she seemed surprised to see me. I wonder what she had heard about me and if it was her that sent Dr Smith here or why he came, will Daa have to pay him, oh Dear I feel as if they tried to keep me in the Dark always will it always be so.*

Through November the entries went on, still filled with ordinary detail and day-to-day information. Catherine sometimes complained of feeling ill and weak, but her writing was neater and her thought clearer. Then on 26 November the writing once more became large and ragged. 'They say I am ill', said Catherine. 'I don't feel very bad. Something takes most of the pain.' The last entry by Catherine was 7 December.

On 9 December 1895, Bert took his mother to Leith's Railway Hotel in Drouin, where she was examined by Doctors Travers and Smith. Both certified that she was a lunatic, and should be detained. Doctor Travers stated in his warrant that the patient 'is under the delusion that her children are better than other people's and that they will be stolen—says that "mischievous fingers" are upon her'.

Doctor Smith noted the 'personal disorders of hair and dress', and delusions about her acquaintances. Bert informed the doctors that she had been unable to sleep, was destructive and 'inclined to break furniture'. On 9 December Catherine Currie was sent to Melbourne, and her brother took her to Yarra Bend. She was admitted for a second time, the diagnosis being delusional insanity.[78]

The diary entries began again on 17 December in a neat new hand, probably Katie's. This was an impersonal record of farm life, and Catherine was never mentioned. Christmas Day is 'very nice and cool. Da and Bert looking for (Carrie) heifer all day. got her but not calved yet. Tom putting up a bail'. There was no mention, as there was in

December 1881, of Catherine being away for Christmas dinner. This time there would be no outpouring of guilt and remorse, no self-recriminations.

1896

In February 1896 Catherine took up her diary again.

21.2   *I am home again, came on evening before yesterday . . . am oh so glad to be home . . . Mr Leggo and his friend here yesterday. I did not see him don't Fancy myself hardly presentable yet.*

She was not well in February, and became really sick in March, and on 9 March complained, 'I suffer more pain than I did all the time I was away just except when they were knocking me about'. By 18 March she had decided she probably had influenza.

Catherine was beaten, but she still would not give up. In March she had an argument with her friend Mrs Cornish about payment for dresses, and in May she was complaining about the Hardie boys. In July she went to see Dr Travers, and the visit brought back bad memories and sleepless nights.

2.7   *I had to get a certificate from the Doctor, that I had ceased to be a Lunatic. O dear it seems awful I have not slept all night, not very much for thinking of it, however I got it. I do hope and pray that this will be the last of that business.*

On 3 July Bert turned twenty-one, and Catherine noted sourly that he was now responsible enough to be put on the electoral roll but that she had been taken off. In September she was suffering from a bad headache.

2.9   *I know the reason of it I am afraid it is my own* fault *but how can*
       I help it. Perhaps if I have more patience I shall be better bye and
       bye God knows I do try but am always misunderstood.

1897

In 1897 Catherine turned fifty-two, but in many ways the year
heralded the beginning of a sad old age. The young, energetic and
ambitious farmer's wife who had begun her life at Lardner with such
hopes for herself and her family had been shut up not once but twice
in a lunatic asylum, and her thoughts were bitter. The respect she
craved had deserted her, even she thought, the respect of her husband
and children.

17.2   *I . . . am of no more consequence than a log of wood—me—that*
       try all I can to make them happier than I was at their age—till I
       married I did not know what happiness was. I never could look
       back to my childhood and wish the Days back again and if John
       had never taken me to a Mad House *I would have been happy in*
       my children . . . but now they seem to wish I was there all the time.
       I have not a friend I can talk to, only my heavenly father—*all I*
       love think me mad.

The children may have had a different version of who had the
hardest time of it. Catherine was still curious and inquisitive, wanting
to know everything and giving advice. In March John was 'swearing at
me', and in April she sat up waiting for her older children to return
home. 'I got no thanks only abuse for sitting up for them' [14.4]. In
August Bert slept in on a cold morning.

26.8   *Took the watering can to get Bert up at last—it was a cold surprise*
       to him this frosty morning, I suppose he will remember all his life.

As dreams of respectability faded, even John was beginning to relinquish his public profile. On 11 August he withdrew his nomination for Council after John Hardie decided to stand against him, and in October his office as a Justice of the Peace lapsed.

1898

The year of 1898 saw Catherine still disappointed in her children.

28.1   *Tom cutting scrub. Says it is very hard will not do any more after tonight. I am very sorry as I don't like to think my Boys think work too hard for them that any other man can do and of course there is work like that done.*

The next day there were other things to worry about when the unoccupied house at Brandie Braes was burnt down in a bushfire. Some of the garden survived, to Catherine's relief, but fires raged through January and February and Catherine noted that she was brought a bottle of brandy, 'as I don't like to be without some these terrible times'.

George Stoving was in Europe, and Catherine wrote to him with news of the disasters. He replied with a long and sympathetic letter, filled with information.

> *I address this letter to you in answer to your lines of 18th of April for which I thank you; I was very glad indeed to get some news and Mr Currie is mistaken if he thinks I don't care for a woman's letters. Yes you must have been very busy all of you with bushfires —what a terrible year for droughts and misfortunes even in Gippsland. I never thought the wattels would escape and am glad*

to hear from you that they have now. Of course the paddocks had to be sown all over again with grass probably even the one near Grants. I read shocking accounts from all sides and if you know people in great want, distribute some of my clothing before the moths eat it—in fact give it all away. I shall have plenty to replace them. The only thing I don't want you to give away are my linen shirts and the yellow fibre jacket which I wear in hot weather— you know. And the starlings are doing well and you have to feed them, a poor job for the girls—still it would be such a blessing if we could make them settle permanently on Yuulong, the only way to get the hoppers under—'more cultivation more grass hoppers' that is a rule for all warm Countries. Mr Gravins says it is the same in South America, only there they have the locusts and that is worse; in Riverina and near Albury the Country was full with grasshoppers even in winter—and we shall be the first to feel them less. But the bushfires will be a recurring evil too and I pity the poor settlers with their dry timber so near their houses—I almost think I would sow wheat in some parts, it will keep a good price for some time and summer is getting drier—the rainfall Mr Spence sends me is beastly low up to now, April only 2½ inch up to 26/4/98. Mr Horsfall writes me that it costs him £200 a week to feed his sheep—it is terrible. Here they have splendid crops and grass fields, the country is at its best like with us in December and everything looks simply perfection. Very rich soil around Leipzig and very high cultivation.

I wonder if we got Lempriere's farm or if it was too late when I cabled; we want a good rich piece of land in those hills—fairly level and not very far. In about 2½ months I shall think of taking my steamer back to Australia and hope to see you all well after all the fire and drought trouble; we shall get the old seasons again I am sure, this drought is excessive and exceptional.

Give my kind regards to Mr Currie for whom this letter is equally intended and to all the rest of the family, the lassies in particular.

Yours very truly,
George Stoving

Letters from Mr Stoving were now one of the few excitements in Catherine's life. There were few outings, and the children were giving her little pleasure, for they did not live up to her expectations. Rose turned fourteen in May of 1898, and Fernie was sixteen in September, and even Catherine's two babies were beginning to demand their independence. In October, Catherine noted,

6.10   *Niether Rose or Fern are playing speaks with me today because they did not get to the Dance last night.*

Later that month Catherine was sure that Rose was trying to deceive her by hiding some of Bert's mail.

20.10   *I wonder why Rose hid the card from me. I don't know my girls at all—I feel sure if a perfect stranger had been there when she opened the mail bag—she would have said one for Bert—then when I told her she said she did not think I was interested which must have been a lie. The reason was she thought I was too much interested—and wished to vex me. She certainly succeeded. I do all I can to please those two girls but they never think of me for a moment but if there is a way that they are sure will vex me that they do. I feel sure they will feel it as they grow older and I am sorry that they should—very sorry indeed.*

1899

In February 1899 Tom set off for New Zealand again. He had gone once before, in February 1897, but had returned four months later. This time, Catherine was more anxious than ever, for John was not well. He was ill in March, and on 14 March had an argument with the workmen, in the course of which he boxed the ears of Perry, one of the workers. He was so upset that he would not come to the table, and Catherine took his dinner to his room. On 30 March Mr Stoving sent a telegram recalling Perry. John turned sixty-five in June, and was not well in July. Finally, on 25 July, the doctor diagnosed that John was suffering from sugar diabetes. In August the family was much relieved to welcome Tom home from New Zealand, for John's health was worsening, and continued to deteriorate throughout the year.

1900

On 3 February 1900 John was 'knocked up' after working alone at the thistles; 'girls blame me for letting him go—but I cant keep him—when he *wishes* to do anything—*never could*—'. On 28 February Catherine noted the engagement of a local couple and remarked 'the parents made the match: very suitable'. She had found no suitable matches for her own children, who were now moving more and more beyond her control. In July Rose said some 'very naughty things' to her mother, rendering Catherine quite ill and unable to do the milking. On 30 December she was angry with Tom when he wished to drive his young neighbours, Florrie and Katie Rintels, home. Catherine recorded almost incoherently,

*I would not let him—but I had to tell Florrie she must not ride, as
Tom was going to mind me but I feel I should have to follow them
down to night had he driven her, as I told him I would be ill but
that did not keep him. What does it matter for old folks. Let them
be ill, young folk don't care. I am more sorry to vex Tom—but he
is not sorry for me, well—certainly neither of my sons ever think of
pleasing thier mother. They have never said yet I will drive you—
or take you for a Drive*

In fact, it was on 2 November that Bert had taken her to a concert, a
big event in her life. 'I do love to hear singing, and how little I have
heard in my life.'

The diary for 1900 ended with hopeful verse that Catherine had
found to copy into her diary.

> *The good we do from motives true
> Will never quite be lost.
> For somewhere in Times distant blue
> We'll gain more from the cost.
> And offt I think a strange surprise
> Will meet us when we gain
> Some diadem that hidden lies
> From deeds we thought in vain.*

1901

But 1901 began as usual. On 5 January John was not well, the young
folk were abusing Catherine, and she was ill all night.

6.1   *My own loved ones were too hard on me, why will they—said I try
to vex them—it was only I was afraid to let Tom drive his sisters to*

the cricket match—with Steele. I have suffered—They do not know—I think if they did they would not be so hard—I feel sure I do not deserve that they should be.

On 19 February she received a letter from her sister-in-law Mrs Wells of South Yarra, telling her that 'they had laid my Father away on Saty—only Annie and Lep, with Carries Husband went'. Her father, aged eighty-two at the time of his death, had not recognised anyone for the past three years.

On 30 March Catherine heard Tom talking 'of taking his bluey and going off somewhere Monday'. As usual, Catherine was hurt at not being told.

It is the old Aboriginal habit, suppose it must be in the air—the old folk should be killed off—they are only in the young ones way, as soon as they think they can do for themselves—they never for one instant think of pleasing their parents—they can manage themself so much better—forgive them Dear Lord and let it not be entered in the great Book against them.

And the next day she had a headache, for 'a sore heart makes a sore head'.

Most of Catherine's worry was for herself, but some was for John, whose health was rapidly failing. In May he grew worse, and by 9 June was confined to bed. Tom came home on 10 June, and two days later the doctor said there was no hope for John's recovery. He died on 15 June.

1.7.1901 *One year today I commenced this Book—what have I to write now? the saddest of all news Dear Daa left me for that Bourne from whence there is no return. I shall go to him but ah he cannot come to me, he was weary here, anxious to go—so we cannot greive as those that have no hope.*

The funeral was well attended, and death notices were placed in both the leading papers on 17 June. There were letters from all parts of the state—'Dear Daa was very highly respected—but none knew how good he really was, as he allways thought least of himself'. Life went on without John, and he was rarely mentioned in the diary. Mr Stoving returned from Europe in October, 'wondering how he would find us without Daa'.

1902

Rose was working as the postmistress at the Lardner Post Office in 1902, a position which would alternate between her and Katie for the next few years. Tom left again for New Zealand in February 1902, and Catherine was doubtful whether Bert would be able to look after them properly.

8.2   *Bert scolding upset me terribly and it was for nothing. I was surprised when he said he wanted to help to put a Tap in the Horse tank—as I did not think he was clever enough for that. He did not take it as I meant it and went great lengths about—I was not surpriesed when he found he could not do it. I hope he felt small, perhaps he did—but not small enough to get inside the Tank.*

On 4 April the bulls broke loose, and Catherine complained, 'oh dear, I feel as tho I could not trust Bert to take care of us'. Catherine was doing her best (or worst) to keep control at Yuulong.

8.4   *Mr Stoving wished to take Hans from the plough to cart posts. I would not let him. Seems very cross about it—but I cant help it. I*

must not let him take the ploughman from the plough when the
master is away—oh Dear—how hard some people makes it for
others to live.

On 27 May the prodigal son returned.

27.5　*Tom is home—walked in last night just when I was wishing for*
him—oh so much . . . I was fretting as Mr Stoving and I had an
unpleasantness about the Gates—he had told Taylor to tar the
entrance Gates—I objected—he said they were his Gates.

The relationship with Stoving was obviously deteriorating. In October
he hired a trap to drive himself from the station; only the second time
he had done so in thirteen years. He should have given the Curries the
money, Catherine thought, for all the times they had driven in for him.
Stoving was now planning to sell Yuulong, and early in 1903 plans
were under way for the family to rebuild at Brandie Braes, and move
back to their own farm.

1903

On 15 January Laura Deacon came to stay, and there was a night of
singing. 'I wonder if anyone who loved singing as I do ever heard so
little good singing', Catherine wondered. Through February, March
and April the house was being built, and by May work had started on
the barn. Bert, who had a team of bullocks, did the carting of the
building materials. On 30 June 1903 Catherine noted that she was at
last about to return to Brandie Braes.

*I am putting away my book trying to get to sleep at B. Braes
tonight. Oh dear I feel very shaky—if we were once away we will
be right how different to when we came. Then I did not feel a
bit concerned, were just going to make a fortune right away.
Mr Stoving said we seem to be leaving it all to him but the boys
have built a nice house and no one will tell us to move on again,
with God's Blessing we shall be better than here and nobody to
find fault with us. Suppose this last Yulong entry.*

The new house was well and solidly built, and on 18 July a cheque for
£100 was paid to the carpenter, the last of three payments. Such a lot of
money, thought Catherine.

There were a few regrets about leaving Yuulong; the cabinet
Mr Stoving had given to John had been taken over by the new house-
keeper, Mrs Taylor. But there were worse regrets at the new Brandie
Braes, all relating to the children Catherine had brought up.

10.9.1903 *Oh dear it is hard to live sometimes. Fern told me yesterday I was
a* hypocrite—*been one all my days, such a thing to say to her
mother—and what makes it harder I believe she really thinks it. Is
it hypocrisy to make the best of what you have and pretend you like
it just to please those you love? I allways said I like to do just what
I was obliged to do, but I can't think thats hypocracy. I allways
said I did just what I liked but then I made myself like what I had
to do with allways a prayer to our Heavenly Guide—for the incli-
nation to do it—that surely can't be* hypocrisy.

15.9 *Katie and I had a controversy today—it seems hard to me. I only
claim to have planted one plant or slip in the garden and she told
me I was taken credit for what I did not do—adding that that was
nothing unusual.*

1904–1908

On 18 January 1904 Fern and Rose were playing no speaks, and Katie took their side against their mother. Catherine remarked:

> *Perhaps they will know they are wrong some day but at present I do not seem to have a friend, certainly not among my own daughters . . . they call it hypocrisy—do they mean it, do they think it. God that seeth into the heart knows I pray for them all time*

However, on 25 February the girls gave their mother a black cashmere dress, eau-de-cologne and slippers for her birthday.

On 11 March, when Mrs Rintels got a piano, Catherine wished for one too.

> *I am sure we will never have one in my lifetime. Perhaps—I hope so. We have many things now that I had given up hopes of. I thank God for all his Blessings. Music is a luxury.*

A clearance sale was held at Yuulong on 23 March, and Bert and Tom made some purchases. The next day the furniture arrived on a dray and Catherine was delighted, although she believed that now they had paid for the things 'twice over', given their service at Yuulong. It was nice, however, to have the familiar things around, and her bedroom properly furnished.

24.3 *. . . it only wants a few months of Forty years that I have been waiting for it, so surely it is my turn now. Dear Daa had allways a notion that we would not make a living and would have to sell things again and they never fetch half what we have to buy them for he said. So we allways put it off and the money went one don't* *know where—I think perhaps it might have been as well if we had got them before.*

Life seemed a bit more peaceful for some months. They were only milking seven cows now, so the workload had also diminished for the women. In August 1905 Fern left to work for her aunt in Dandenong for ten shillings a week, and Catherine was in favour of the arrangement, thinking it would do her good. But in September she returned, as Auntie's business was falling away, and she could no longer employ her. There were still fights with the 'children' as Catherine called the adults living in her house; in January she argued with Bert, and in December it was Rose who was causing trouble.

16.12   *Rose lost her temper and refused to do what I asked her to . . . oh she frightened me—I tried to frighten her too but I could not. I would have poured a half bucket of milk over her—only I thought it would take her so long to wash it out of her hair . . . both Fern and her make me afraid for them—it will be better if they never never got married or they will certainly figure in the police court for their husband knocking them about—they love nobody—and only think of themselves and one eggs on the other—I don't know what to do with them oh it was* horrible *the things Rose said to me tonight I don't feel I shall ever forget it—what shall I Do.*

She had such a headache the next day that she could not go to church, but stayed at home to ponder where she had erred.

Catherine was too anxious to write in early 1906 as the year began with fires. In April it was decided that Fern should go to work as cook and housemaid for Mr Strickland; she would stay for a month on trial.

1.4   *She makes it all much harder for everybody here as she will not be contented with what we can do for her and everybody in the house tries to please* her *but she will not see that it is so.*

In May and June Fern came home to visit, looking very happy, but in July Rose was ill and Catherine had a sore leg, and sent for Fern. She arrived home on 12 July, and Catherine was 'very glad'. She could not live with her children, but she hated it when they were away from home. By 22 October she was once again fighting with the girls; they had disagreed with her about treatment for Bert's sore foot, and even worse, had not shown her what they had bought when they had been out shopping.

January 1907 saw a fight with Rose, February a fight with Fern after she had abused the men for being late for dinner—'She frightens me as I beleive she Hates her mother' [28.2]. Catherine still kept careful track of the children, sitting up to wait for them when they went out at night, and recording their arrivals and departures. But after the first two months there were fewer fights. Catherine's energy was flagging. On 28 December an entry by Katie recorded that Mother was ill. The 1908 entries proceeded in Katie's hand throughout January, with no mention of Mother. In February there were fires, and Mother was worse, and the family sent for the doctor.

On 9 March Katie recorded that Doctor Cowens could give no hope of recovery, and the next entry read:

> *Mother passed to her rest on the 10th March. She did not know anyone for the last 24 hours and we can only hope she was in no pain. When will we manage to do without her, the place seems so lonely now and there is not the same sympathy about it. 'For her far better'. All the aunts and uncles came to see us and sympathise with us. At least they gave us more to do and break us in to our sorrow.*

The diary continues, with little further mention of Catherine. On 10 May the will was read in favour of Tom Currie.

Epitaph

Life went on, as it does after every definitive ending. Tom and Bert worked together at their sawmill as well as on the farm, and Bert took carting contracts around the district with his bullock team. Katie planted another beautiful garden around Brandie Braes, as her mother had taught her, with stands of beech trees around the property and roses in the garden. Rose and Fern joined the Drouin Golf Club, where Mr Stoving's lessons proved valuable. In the 1920s the Curries bought some more land, purchasing O'Keefe's former property.[79]

It was Bert who left the farm to marry and start his own family, possibly after some sort of altercation. This may have been about his failure to keep the pact of remaining single and childless, and he and his wife had two children, a boy and a girl. These would be Catherine's only grandchildren. Bert had always been, or so it seemed, the outsider. The middle child among the surviving children, he was separated by six years from the older siblings, and by seven years from his two younger sisters. It was Bert who was closest in age to the drowned sister, and it was Bert who was singled out by his mother for derision and punishment. It was he who did most for Catherine around the farm, taking charge when favourite son Tom went away. It was Bert who gave his evidence to the doctor in order to have Catherine admitted to an asylum, and who bore the costs of this.

Epitaph

Bert died in 1933 at the age of fifty-eight. This son, the one most often derided and scorned by Catherine, perhaps the son she most depended upon, decided to live his own life beyond the farm, and to create his own family. The others were left, as Catherine may have wished, with the mission to preserve their parents' myth.

On 26 March 1939, more than thirty years after Catherine's death, twenty-five visitors from the Naturalists Society arrived at Brandie Braes to admire the results of her life of hard work. Some came by train and some by car, a smooth journey now from Melbourne. Fern recorded the visit, and once more took the opportunity to note that bad luck in selecting the land had made their lives more difficult:

> Following Lardner's Track, unrecognizable now through helpful deviations, the party entered the farm of 'Brandie Braes' . . .
>
> Another mile and we reached the homestead where this pioneer family have built homes since 1875, when the parents first started on the herculean (and heart-breaking) task of mastering the forest. This has never been done because we were just off the Hazel (*Pomadernis*) [*sic*] country which, when burnt, grew only grass. But ours—with its Acacias (*A. verticillata*), Prickly Moses, and *A. stricla* [*sic*] (Hop Acacia) grew again and again if left alone. Before Drouin or Warragul were formed (1878), we went to Melbourne by road, horse and dray, over such roads, twice a year.
>
> A very large chestnut tree remains in the first garden of the district, planted in 1876. Here are remnants of huge Cherry trees, the joy of our youth; a row of Corsican (Nut) pine trees and a clump of *Euc. globulus*; one of two patches sown in 1886, surely unusual when trees were everywhere. Very many orchids have been found on the farm, subject to seasonal conditions. During the cycle of hot dry summers, our world was a barren place; but following the wet cycle, we would get great numbers, and unusual variety and size. Lyre-birds were plentiful; Magpies followed the clearing of the land; also Parrots. The poor Koalas suffered cruelly at holiday time when city visitors showed their want of skill with a gun. Bower-birds by the hundred ate everything grown in the vegetable garden if left

173

alone, and Possums and flying Phalangers (four species) worked the bush at night.

Meanwhile, the clearing went on despite bad years, drought conditions, bank failing (1893), and bush fire depredations (there were no relief funds then), until both 'Brandie Braes' and the neighbouring 'Yuulong' (where we rented for 14 years), were the lovely homes they are now.

That our happy hunting grounds for native flora were spoilt by the entrance of the rabbit in 1903, and their following hunters, whose attraction is also larger game, is the natural outcome of the different phase of labour conditions. Today's writers on fauna destruction all blame the early settlers for the destruction of our native flora and fauna. This is incorrect. Following the land owner there is always a class eager to pick up easy money with the help they can get from the conditions prevailing. We have suffered from this for sixty-two years, and more acutely today when motor cars make it easy for the aggressors.

C. C. Currie

One of the naturalists put a little postscript to this account from Caroline Calphurnia:

> Every member of the party has a pleasant memory of the Lardner excursion. The Misses Currie and their brother made it a happy day for us. We were entertained in the true Gippsland manner . . . Our thanks to our hosts, who could not have been kinder or more thoughtful to make the excursion enjoyable for everybody.— C.B.[80]

The Misses Currie presumably included Katie and Rose as well as Fern. Katie and Tom were in their seventies, and Fern and Rose were in their fifties when they conducted the naturalists about their house, garden and paddocks, reflecting once more on their status as a proud pioneer family. The land was their inheritance and their contribution to posterity.

Eventually Fern survived to inhabit the house until her death in 1968 at the age of eighty-six. Unable in her old age to continue running the farm, she employed a manager to run it for her, and then left it to him in her will. He sold it some time later and moved to Western Australia. Bert's children, Catherine and John's only direct descendants, were not considered as possible recipients of the family property.

Catherine was now part of the history which gave meaning to the land, revered for the work she had done in a way that she had not been honoured in life. The epitaph which Fern would give her was an account of the things she had planted and nurtured; this was accompanied by a defence of the pioneers' effect on the landscape. Catherine now had a gravestone with her name on it, as well as a park and a lane named after her family. There was no longer an absence of ghosts, but a throng of presences that had left 'signs of their passing and spaces still warm with breath'.

The pioneers had cut new props to hold up the sky, and they had introduced a new cosmogony to the ancient forest, bringing new voices to its silence. Catherine was a child of the colony but her schooling, parents and husband would have taught her the wider vocabulary and inheritance, an understanding of the sacred canopy under which she lived. She knew about the value of the story. Stories, even lists made in diaries, had a purpose and a weight, a chronology and a moral purpose that would make sense of the world. The covers of a book would enclose these certainties, even at the boundaries of a foreign land that had begun with different narratives.

At the beginning of a story, as at the beginning of a life, it appears that all options are still open. It is only with hindsight that the ending appears to be inevitable. It becomes apparent that every word chosen excludes another, every action taken will have its own consequences, every cause will have its effect, leading to the given end. Catherine's diary is a primary document, and it has the immediacy of life. It is written without knowledge of the end.

As the survivors and inheritors of the story, we are also its interpreters and we will make a different story. Our cosmogony, like Catherine's, still concerns taxonomies of time. But the props that held up the sky, the supports for the sacred canopy, have been removed as surely as the forest has been cut down. We have altered the boundaries, and now we are surrounded by uncertainty, fragmentation, and a break in the narrative. Our somewhat less than sacred canopy covers a land now filled with a variety of dreams.

The Australia we inhabit is a fabulist land of strange animals and venomous spiders and snakes, where modern legends grow from tales of dingoes carrying away soft white babies who should never have been placed in wild red places so inimical to matinee jackets. Such stories no longer seem foreign, and this is as much a result of our time as of our place. For Catherine is now also part of our history, and we know that children will drown in wells and mothers will go mad, in spite of good intentions and with no apparent moral purpose. We no longer believe in happy endings, or in the calm progression of the story.

Our modern philosophy consists of the knowledge that progress is based on unpredictable mutations, and that variety and not certainty is the engine of evolution. A physicist who speculates about extending the theory of evolution to the whole cosmos has said, 'What was once thought to be absolute is always subject to evolution and re-negotiation . . . the complete truth about the world is not graspable as any single point of view, but only resides in the totality of several or many distinct views'.[81] Every point of view, each person's narrative, now contributes to the story and Catherine has become part of that larger story. If language is 'the mode of heredity outside the genes',[82] Catherine's diary has made her a survivor. The boundaries of her life are now enclosed within the covers of those books, written in her own hand and, at a further remove, within the limits of this one. The diary is Catherine's own production, now mediated by us for our own purposes. Reading between the lines, commenting from the perspective of our own time and place, we make subjective judgements informed by our own experiences and our own wish to find, within the grand panorama, the faint colour of human happiness.

Like a true survivor, Catherine has left a vestige of herself, and from behind the boundary that separates past and present her words echo to colour our perceptions of her life and our own. We may no longer be allowed to believe, as she once did, that life can be organised and structured into certain meaning, but her life is part of the history that has taught us the modern mistrust of both happiness and certainty.

Gippsland, it seems, is a good place to generate uncertainty— somewhere at the fringe, on the boundary of the land, green and beautiful and close to the sapphire blue where sharks circle. A modern poet has left a Gippsland epitaph which could belong to Catherine as well as to her translators:

> For no clear reason we ache
> To shape of imprecision certain knowledge;
> But things won't integrate, though birds glide
> Like thoughts at the fringe of vision's unshaped words.[83]

Appendix 1: Origins

Sarah Ann Catherine Wells was born in the port town of Ipswich in south-east England on 25 February 1845. Her birth certificate recorded only her first two names, although by the time she married nineteen years later, Catherine had been added. She was the second child of Leaper Harry (often listed as Hurry) Wells and Elizabeth, née Parish, residents of St Helen's Street. This street was the home and the workplace of many of the trades and crafts that helped make Ipswich a prosperous and expanding town at the time of Catherine's birth. It supplied all the commodities needed by its rich and extensive agricultural hinterland, and also shipped the foodstuffs produced inland around the coast to London.

In St Helen's Street there were carpenters, a cooper, cordwainer, mill-wright, confectioner, dressmaker, and two brickmakers, one of whom was Catherine's father Leaper. It was an industrious and lively street of self-employed workers who were comfortable but not affluent. Most had large families packed into their modest houses. The south side of the street was dominated by the large county gaol, while St Helen's church towered above the north side. Catherine's earliest landscape was dominated by these twin symbols of the goodness and the fallibility of humanity.

Catherine's mother Elizabeth had spent some of her childhood in St Helen's Street. She was the third daughter of Joshua Parish, the innkeeper at the Duke of York, and his wife Maria. Both parents were forty years old at the time of the 1841 census, and had ten living children in addition to Elizabeth. This was a large family even by the standards of early nineteenth-century England, when child mortality had begun to fall while birth rates remained at their high pre-industrial levels. Leaper had been born in Ipswich in 1819, the eldest of three children of Leaper Robert Wells, a carpenter. He met and courted Elizabeth while she lived at the inn and they were married in St Helen's Church on 6 August 1841 when she was eighteen and he was twenty-four. They began married life in the street where they had grown up, and Leaper continued to work as a brickmaker.

Brickmaking was an important craft in Suffolk because of the county's lack of building stone and reliance on brick as the main building material. The work required skill as well as physical labour. Clay was dug from a pit and carted to the brickyard, where it was mixed with water in a wash mill until it broke up into a slurry. This allowed pebbles and other unwanted matter to fall to the bottom. The mills were often operated by a horse which circled while dragging a harrow, a device which Leaper would later see in use on the goldfields of Victoria. (In the Antipodes it was the heavy gold, not the unwanted matter, which fell to the bottom of the mill.) The purified slurry dried out in large pits until it reached a butter-like consistency for moulding into bricks. The green bricks were stacked to dry out before being fired in a kiln to emerge as the distinctive cream-coloured bricks still seen in houses throughout Suffolk.

Brickmaking was a seasonal occupation because frosts caused the moisture in green bricks to freeze, splitting and crumbling them so that they could not be fired. Ipswich brickmakers traditionally found winter work in the maltings close to the River Orwell, along which the barley for malting was shipped. Leaper may have found warm work there in the winter months, as the maltings were only a short walk from his home in St Helen's Street. For the rest of the year he made bricks, possibly as a wage-labourer, but more probably in partnership with one or two other men, using a rented clay pit and kiln. Leaper and the five other brickmakers were manufacturing the fabric of the rapidly growing town. Bricks were generally in demand, but the building industry was volatile, swinging from boom to slump as the trade cycle ran its course.[84]

By 1851 Leaper and Elizabeth had left St Helen's Street. They had exchanged busy Ipswich and its 30 000 inhabitants for the tiny village of Monks Eleigh, fifteen miles west of Ipswich in the vale of the river Brett. With eldest daughter Elizabeth and six-year-old Catherine there was now four-year-old George and another child on the way. Monks Eleigh had 700 inhabitants and a handful of craftsmen, and Leaper was probably operating the brickyard on a large agricultural estate, supplying bricks for barns and other buildings as the estate expanded. Bricks were too heavy to transport far, and it was common to set up a brickyard close to the source of demand.

Monks Eleigh was not too far from Ipswich, and the local newspaper, the *Ipswich Journal*, arrived every week. In 1851 it brought dramatic news from the world outside Suffolk. There was fighting in South Africa, revolutionary upheaval in Paris, a mighty international exhibition in London and gold discoveries in Australia. Edward Hammond Hargraves's early find near Bathurst in New South Wales was reported in Ipswich on 6 September 1851, almost six months after the event. Other more detailed reports continued to reach rural Suffolk, and by the end of the year the government of newly independent Victoria was offering assisted passages to tempt migrants to the southern colony.

Early in 1852 news of the massive Victorian finds completely eclipsed the New South Wales fields. There were reports of diggers earning £20–100 a day, and of vast quantities of gold being brought to

Melbourne from three fields each week. There were also reports of a lack of water and of epidemics on the Mount Alexander diggings. Despite this, it was reported that thousands of colonists were deserting their jobs to try their luck with pick and shovel. Positions remained unfilled despite the offer of wages at a scale unknown in England. New fields were being discovered, and it seemed that Victoria's stores of gold were inexhaustible.

Such news may have been difficult to comprehend for the Suffolk labourers patiently following the age-old patterns of work in order to scrape a meagre living. They had heard similar stories three years earlier, when the first chaotic gold rush in California had been reported, but now it was stressed that the Victoria rushes were peaceful and lawful. The newspaper carried inducements to migrate; apart from the obvious lure of gold and the assisted passages provided by the Victorian Government, shippers advertised for migrants and listed their frequent sailing dates to Victoria. During a visit to England, John Fairfax, editor of the *Sydney Morning Herald*, described the type of migrant required:

> To the young man of industrious and sober habits and of moral character, whose anxiety is to pursue a course of honest perseverance—unappalled by difficulty and danger—I say go. To the idle, the dissipated, and the drunken—he who is reckless alike of his own peace and the sorrow he causes to others—I say stay; for if you go to a warm climate and persevere in your present habits, you will be an outcast, you will die miserably, neglected by man, and, perhaps, unpitied by God. The two great wants of the colonies are capital and labour.[85]

This was a 'memorable era' on both sides of the world, with the new Crystal Palace and the Great Exhibition in London matched by the discovery of gold in Australia.

Leaper Wells must have thought long and hard about the gold-fields of Australia. Like many working men, he would have been more attracted to the lure of golden Victoria than to the industrial England represented at the Great Exhibition. If he could not make a fortune on the goldfields of Australia, he would be able to find work in an economy desperately short of workers. Certainly he was well equipped for the task: young and strong and accustomed to hard labour with a shovel. He was also familiar with the soil, with its variety and characteristics. He had already shown a willingness to move in search of work. He stood out from the majority of gold seekers only in his willingness to take his wife and large family with him on his adventure.

Regular reports from Victoria continued to appear in the *Ipswich Journal* into 1853. Most confirmed the view of one correspondent that 'without doubt, Australia is the most extraordinary country on the globe for resources'.[86] One digger struck a discordant note in describing how he and many others had been robbed by bushrangers on the Ballarat to Melbourne road. He was about to turn his back on gold and return home to England because there was no 'comfort' in Victoria, and because there were few jobs except in the building trades.[87] This probably came too late for Leaper, who had already booked a passage for himself and his family.

At the beginning of May 1853, Catherine began her journey to the new continent. Her father was thirty-four and her mother twenty-eight, and they took nine-year-old Elizabeth, seven-year-old Catherine, six-year-old George, four-year-old Alida and two-year-old Henry Leaper. At Plymouth they boarded the *Calphurnia*, a barque of 750 tons, which sailed on 15 May carrying just over 200 passengers, 200 cases of spirits and 250 cases of beer. The vessel had already done a round trip to Melbourne the previous year. Under Captain Green it took almost three months to reach its destination, finally dropping anchor on 13 August 1853 in Hobson's Bay, which was already crammed with shipping from all over the world. Official records tell us no more of Catherine until her marriage to John Currie eleven years on. In the intervening years she acquired an education, and could read, write and do arithmetic. She was now a colonist, having spent her most formative years in Victoria.

John Currie arrived in Hobson's Bay in 1854, one year after the Wells family. However, he would not be a child of the colony as Catherine was, for he was already twenty years old. John had been born on 11 June 1834 in West Calder, Midlothian, Scotland, to Thomas and Elizabeth Currie (formerly Bryce). He was their third child. His mother had died by the time the census enumerator found him in 1841 living with his father and twelve-year-old sister Catherine Jean. James, it appeared, had already left home.*

John booked a passage on the *Champion of the Seas* which sailed from Liverpool on 10 November 1854 with nearly 900 passengers bound for Melbourne. It arrived the day before Christmas after a record-breaking passage of only 72 days. The mighty clipper ship of 3000 tons was the largest ship to have entered Port Phillip Bay, dwarfing the hundred or so other vessels lying to anchor in Hobson's Bay near the entrance of the Yarra River. According to the Melbourne *Argus*, this was the noblest and most elegant of ships, which had travelled 465 miles in one 24-hour period, and had averaged 199 miles per day for the whole trip.[88]

This trip to Australia remained a highlight of John's life. Passengers were so pleased with Captain Newland's command that they placed paid advertisements in the papers in praise of him. They were probably less pleased when port authorities quarantined the ship for three days because of a smallpox outbreak during the trip. John spent

---

* On John's death certificate his father's name is given as James, but all other evidence points to him as Thomas. There may have been some confusion by surviving relatives with the name of his elder brother James. It is possible that his mother may have died in childbirth, but we have been unable to find details of her death, which took place before civil registration of births, deaths and marriages became mandatory in Scotland.

his twentieth Christmas on a ship anchored off Williamstown, the goldfields still tantalisingly beyond his reach.

Victoria's golden treasure, extensive as it was, could never have satisfied the desires of those who flocked to find it. Too many came with too little capital, knowledge and skills. The information which Leaper Wells had read in his local paper was accurate, but it was dangerously outdated by the time it reached him, six months after the event. By the time he and others like him had acted upon the information and reached the diggings, nearly a year had elapsed and the goldfields had grown to staggering proportions. By the end of 1853 when Leaper reached the diggings there were 53 000 inhabitants; the number had grown to 100 000 two years later.

As more and more people arrived, the areas with rich alluvial gold near the surface were rapidly exhausted. A miner was allowed to stake only a small claim measuring twelve feet by twelve feet. The small area was quickly worked out, and the miner moved on to a new claim, perhaps on a newly discovered field. There were increasingly frantic rushes to new fields, with thousands arriving a few days after hearing a rumour, competing for space along the creeks. Many found some gold, but soon realised that it was at the cost of incessant labour, frequent movement and uncertainty, and the knowledge that very few found enough gold to relieve them from labour permanently.

Leaper and Elizabeth would have found the life extremely hard with their large family of young children. We do not know how long they stayed on the goldfields, but it may have been only a few weeks. At some stage Leaper went back to his craft of brickmaking. Like many others he realised that a better living could be made by supplying the rapidly growing economy with building materials. Housing was vital for a population which expanded sevenfold in the 1850s, a rate of increase only ever experienced in a gold-rush climate. The Victorian census of 1861 discovered that a third of Victorians were living in temporary accommodation ten years after gold had first been discovered.

Leaper and his family settled in the picturesquely located small town of Bacchus Marsh on the road from Melbourne to the Ballarat diggings. Catherine was probably living here by December 1854 and would have watched the large contingent of troops passing through on their way to Ballarat to fight against the diggers at the Eureka Stockade. She was certainly there in 1862 when a diphtheria epidemic struck, killing many of the children she knew.[89] By 1865 Bacchus Marsh had a population of 500, with another 1500 living in the immediate agricultural district. There were around 450 houses, some of which were built with the bricks made by Leaper, three flour mills, a brewery and three stone quarries. By 1855 Leaper had become sufficiently prosperous to contribute £2 10s—equivalent to two weeks of a labourer's wage—towards a fund for the construction of what became known as the Iron School. Catherine attended this school with children from the Grant, Hamilton and Walsh families. Cornelius Cunningham, later to marry Jane, was also a scholar.

John Currie also left the goldfields and moved back to his former skills, and in his case it was land which offered him an alternative living. By the end of 1856 John's elder brother James had joined him in the colony, and between this year and 1863 he had made the transition from mining the land to cultivating it. The records show that he was paying rates on 120 acres of land he was renting near Ballan in this year. He may have found enough gold to finance his ambition to become a farmer, and he selected 90 acres of land at Parwan, near Bacchus Marsh, later transferred to the name of a neighbouring farmer. In 1864 he married Catherine Wells, and in December 1865 he selected another 114 acres at Ballan in the Parish of Gorong.

It was to this selection, Woodmuir, that Catherine and John moved with their first child. Elizabeth Bryce Currie had been born in May

1865, but tragedy struck when she died of inflammation of the throat just before her first birthday. In April 1867 Catherine (Kate) was born, followed in August 1869 by Thomas Bryce (Tom). Catherine would bear seven children in all, the average number for a woman of her generation. The great adventure, the journey from the Old Country to the new, had now settled down to a routine of domesticity and extremely hard work.

Appendix 2: Diagnosis
by Garry Sheehan

Most people will live ordinary lives and, when their friends and children have died and no living soul remembers them, they die except as part of the nation's records. Catherine Currie is exceptional because she lives on through her diary. Furthermore, she is known in a way few people can be known. She suffered two psychotic illnesses which allow her to be known in sickness as well as in health. Those episodes, their development and the aftermaths, are documented in the diary and in Yarra Bend Asylum records.

The diary provides information upon which comment can be made about the genesis of psychiatric illness. It begins as a record of farming life, with little of the personal dimension revealed. However, even this daily record becomes relevant, with hindsight, once Catherine's more personal reflections in later years are taken into account. These diaries carry enough of Catherine's inner world to be able to establish many of her unwritten rules. Part of the contribution

---

* Dr Garry Sheehan, a psychoanalyst who is also a psychiatrist, offers this interpretation of our interpretation. He has focused upon those parts of the diary and of our book that touch on Catherine's illness.

of psychoanalysis is to reveal to people a knowledge of their personal myths, and to release them from the bonds of other people's myths. Catherine's diary in its early stages can be read not only as a daily farm record, but as an indication of how her inner world and rules for living were already manifesting themselves.

Catherine can be known in detail around several axes. These were work, relationships, and her usual emotional states. The axis most prominent in the diary has to do with work. She hated 'idleness'. So the first rule which appears and runs like a red thread throughout her life can be stated as: 'Daily work shall always take priority over relationships'. Work was her life, and she did not want it interrupted by friends and neighbours. Life was a never-ending series of jobs to be done or demands to be met. Work was everywhere but it carried with it the danger of indebtedness. Catherine was an efficient trader and barterer, but in sharing work with neighbours she felt put into their debt. This is inevitable, for there are some forms of help and kindness which can never be repaid, and we must accept unpayable debt such as to parents or to a spouse. Catherine hated being in such a position. She preferred to be distant and disdainful of people and what they offered.

Through work we gain a glimpse of her experience of relationships. Throughout her life she felt slighted by people; early in life by neighbours, but later in life by her children. Why was she so vulnerable to slight, real or imagined? She felt put upon and exploited if others asked for help, striving for her ideal of self-sufficiency and always trying to avoid indebtedness. Perhaps part of the answer was her outrage with people. They became 'impudent', abusive and an unwanted burden which interrupted the work. She seemed happier in relationships with animals and children. Her perception of impudence and slights was a sore point in the home, because John would attempt to explain perceived impudence as ignorance without malicious intent. He attempted to placate her, and yet the feeling of being slighted continued throughout her life. She continually found proof in the attitude of others that she did not have much worth.

The heavy emphasis in the diary on John's doings indicates that Catherine's life was lived for him, and in his shadow. Censorship was another of her rules and, just as she did not confide John's impressions of Gippsland to her diary, we can assume that many impressions were censored if they did not meet some standard or other. Life was lived by recording John's work and interests, and Catherine appeared to see herself as his amanuensis. This tells us something important and dangerous. She had such a tenuous and conditional self worth that life's vicissitudes might demand too much of her, and this lack of worth could prove crucial.

From the core of her being Catherine was under the sway of a number of emotional states. These led her to hold beliefs in life which found socially acceptable forms of expression. However, the deep unconscious roots to the beliefs were never adequately resolved. This and life's events led to psychotic episodes later in life. The first emotional belief was her sense of impending danger. The dangers were always threatening to run out of control, like the bushfires every summer, wild animals and vermin. There was a desperate need to hold control for fear of what might erupt. These fears grew larger and became personal; while Catherine was beside herself about the bushfires and desperate to find a buyer and leave, John would go off the next day on a visit to the Exhibition in Melbourne. He did not share her sense of danger.

The dangers in Catherine's mind were how close was death and how close she was to being left alone. She had two solutions to this danger of abandonment. Neighbours and relatives who were difficult to control were cut adrift. With her children she exercised discipline and control which were only part born of maternal concern. As their lives unfolded, she was desperate to hold them to her side even when they were adults.

The second emotional belief which dominated her life was about impoverishment. The desire which Catherine expressed for nice things, a pretty house and more singing in her life were reflections on its internal dullness and tedium. She compensated for this poverty of internal liveliness by living her life through John, and later through her children. She had a sense of herself as devalued and unable to be improved. What could only be inferred from the early diary entries is said without disguise later in life: 'No one cares', 'Not valued by my family', 'like dirt under their feet'.

The death of her baby in 1880 gives a stark view of her internal world, and she did not recover from the death of the child. Her work routine was no longer a defence against such psychic turmoil. In July 1881 her grief had taken a serious turn into psychiatric illness. Catherine felt unwell and lonely, and diagnosed laziness, as that was all she could conceive would lead to idleness. By September her symptoms indicate bipolar disease, with manic element to the fore. Manic features include elation, anger and increased mental speed—flight of ideas, puns, inability to sleep or cease activities. Neglect of eating and tiredness lead to loss of weight. With the elation comes self-confidence, a lack of self-criticism and lack of insight into the illness. Delusions of grandeur are part of the picture. Manic-depressive illness has a 1 to 2 per cent incidence, women predominate and the peak age is thirty to fifty. Genetic factors play a part, with children having a 15 to 20 per cent risk of suffering from the disease. However, nurture effects play a large part in this inheritance.

At the time, mania was the prevalent diagnosis, and probably any agitated state would qualify as mania. Gross forms of mania such as florid mania with delusions could be recognised, but more subtle disturbances could not be detected, partly because of lack of education but also because of lack of effective treatment and isolation. Doctors knew about syphilis and the various forms of madness following physical disease, and they knew about alcoholism and other forms of brain damage. It was only in the 1890s that Freud lead the investigation into the psychological causes of madness, and these theories would take thirty years to find favour in the general community.

John, in searching for answers to her state, decided that love was the panacea, and that he had simply not supplied enough, a normal recrimination for the bewildered guilty. It is noted in the diary that the cold wind of depression and guilt had not reached John, for he somehow sheltered from it and was able to work on. His unavailability to accept some of the emotional aftermath of the tragedy left the burden on Catherine. Two months after her hospitalisation and around the anniversary of the drowning, the wind containing responsibility, depression and guilt finally touched him. Now he started to blame himself, and spoke of his wife with understanding and compassion; she was a good mother and did her best for her child. She had tried to save him from guilt, self-blame and depression, and had lost her sanity in the process. Actually, how much she was sparing him, and how much he was hiding as opposed to being sheltered, is debatable.

The other major casualty in the family was Bert. He had a fairly classical school phobia and all that it meant in light of his mother's illness, his fear of death and her need to keep him near her. Through all this time he was bearing the brunt of maternal decompensation. He was an oedipal child for whom death of some sort is a possibility, but his sad mood and broken heart could not be tolerated. For both Catherine and Bert, a monstrous depression was always about to jump out and get them.

Although Catherine did not mention the Yarra Bend experience until twelve years later, the illness and hospitalisation left a deep scar and she never made peace with the experience. While a holiday trip in September 1895 is ostensibly the start of the next illness episode, her underlying personality predisposition and the changes in her life again put unbearable pressures on her psychological stability. In November 'boys make me wild ... treat their mother as though here on Sufferance', 'Afraid to be near either of them when their father is not here and I am jealous of their smiles to others'. The storm of feelings about her sons, now men, was clear. She had been unable to resolve her feelings about them, and wanted them to remain as tractable little boys so that she could be the only woman in their lives.

As her mind became more disorganised, so too did the writing in the diary. It was large and ragged as she grappled with inevitable disaster, 'They say I am ill', 'I don't feel very bad', 'something takes most of the pain'. The something that stopped her feeling bad was another alteration of reality, another misperception and misunderstanding of the world inside and the world outside.

In December 1895 she was certificated with an illness like the first, with violence and insomnia and again a manic veneer over depression. The content of the delusions was telling. Dr Travers wrote, 'Is under the delusion that her children are better than other people's, and that they will be stolen. Says that "mischievous fingers" are upon her'. In part this grandiosity was an attempt to rationalise the 'theft' of her babies; she was not to blame and it was certainly not because she did not value her children. Conversely, they left because they did not value her. She preferred the delusional belief of their theft rather than the belief that she was not good or attractive enough to keep them at her side. The normal developmental step which parents take of raising children and then allowing them to leave was not possible for Catherine. 'Stolen' carried with it the need for continual vigilance with no rest or distraction from the task. The 'mischievous fingers' could have been the hand of Satan, or fate. She had no insight to internal conflicts causing the problems.

By February 1897 she writes of being 'of no more consequence than a log of wood'. This and similar thoughts earlier are the depressive core of feelings of uselessness and worthlessness which, when intolerable, lead to a manic swing. The harshness of the attacks she can launch on herself are revealed by the kind she can launch on Bert. There is a cruelty in her which, when self-directed, lead to attacks on her self-worth and her reality testing. Her February 1902 attack on Bert was a realistic assessment at best. She unerringly threw cold water on this son and kept him small, for she was unable to let her children grow up and maybe grow away. The irony is that she underestimated with the baby a child's capacity to be independent and to get away from her.

Right up until she died she was recording their arrivals and departures still, just as the diary recorded in earlier years the farm produce and tools lent to neighbours. She was forever attempting to control the world around her, including the people. It is as though they would confer a circle of protection, so that all would be well.

Notes

1 See Duggan, *The Ash Range*, p. 52.
2 Mead, 'Topopoesis', p. 29.
3 'The Satellites Garden', p. 48.
4 Mead, 'Topopoesis', p. 27.
5 Duggan, *The Ash Range*, p. 11.
6 Ibid., p. 9.
7 Malcolm, *The Silent Woman*, p. 100.
8 'Dialogue with a Cruel Partner', pp. 42–3.
9 *Concise Oxford Dictionary*, 5th edition, 1964, 'gold'.
10 See Bullock and Stallybrass, *The Fontana Dictionary of Modern Thought*, p. 410.
11 Monod, *Chance and Necessity*, pp. 102–18.
12 Perhaps the best account of the Selection Acts is to be found in Powell, *The Public Lands of Australia Felix*.
13 'The Rural Myth and the New Urban Frontier', p. 3.
14 *Arcady in Australia*, p. 2.
15 'The Rural Myth and the New Urban Frontier', p. 4.
16 Quoted in Williams, 'More and Smaller is Better', p. 75.
17 For example, see Wilde, *Forests Old, Pastures New*, pp. 29–30; Butler, *Buln Buln*, pp. 429–30
18 Information about John's selections from Land Department Files, 299/19.20.
19 See Butler, *Buln Buln*, p. 205.
20 Quoted in ibid., p. 428.
21 Dawkins, *River out of Eden*, p. 2.
22 'Biography: Self and Sacred Canopy', p. 64.
23 Merquior, *Foucault*, p. 36.
24 *The Order of Things*, p. 380.

[25] Copeland, *The Path of Progress*, p. 208.

[26] Obituary in *Bacchus Marsh Express*, 26 January 1878.

[27] See Butler, *Buln Buln*, p. 374, and Copeland, *Path of Progress*, p. 354.

[28] Details on improvements to the two properties from Land Department Files, John Currie 299/19.20, James Currie 300/19.20.

[29] *Australian Religions*, p. 60.

[30] Mulvaney and White (eds), *Australians to 1788*, Introduction, p. xv. People have been living in Australia for over 40 000 years.

[31] Wilde, *Forests Old, Pastures New*, pp. 6, 10.

[32] *The Ash Range*, p. 24. Laurie Duggan has described his work as 'the poem containing history', and says of his use of sources, 'I have not hesitated to meddle with texts; editing them down, altering the grammar, restructuring sentences, in the interests of clarity; but I have not attempted to pervert the authors' intentions as far as I could perceive them,' (p. 265). His poem of Aboriginal thoughts and feelings would not be based on any text.

[33] Attributed to W. B. Clarke, December 1851: Duggan, *The Ash Range*, pp. 89–90.

[34] Letter by W. A. Brodribb to *Australasian*, 11 May 1878. Quoted in Cuthill, 'The Gippsland Road 1836–1848'.

[35] Attenborough, *The Private Life of Plants*, pp. 34–8 describes the mountain ash as the tallest tree in the world. The effect of fire is described on pp. 132–7: 'If the great trees die from old age before flames have cleared the ground for their seedlings, then they will leave no successors. Paradoxically, such a forest will not survive unless much of it is first destroyed.' *The Land of the Lyrebird* gives types and heights of trees, p. 20.

[36] Quoted in Wilde, *Forests Old, Pastures New*, from 'The Reminiscences of David Brown written in 1924 at the request of The Warragul Shire President Cl. E. R. Jones'. Typescript. Photocopy in West Gippsland library local history collection.

[37] Coverdale, 'The Scrub', pp. 25–6.

[38] Quoted in Butler, *Buln Buln*, p. 201. Butler gives his source as a letter to the Lands Department, *c.* 1967, but we have not located this letter.

[39] Butler, *Buln Buln*, p. 28.

[40] Malouf, 'Space, Writing and Historical Identity: David Malouf talks to Paul Carter about *The Road to Botany Bay*', pp. 102–3. In his book, Paul Carter says, 'The act of settling was not a matter of marking out pre-existing boundaries, but one of establishing symbolic enclosures. It depended on establishing a point of view with a back and front, a place with a human symmetry, a human focus of interest. Boundaries were the means of expressing this ambition, of articulating presence. They represented acts of spatial translation, which did not exclude but set up a dialogue

with the outside environment they created. Hence the widespread destruction and silencing of the bush was not necessarily intentional.' *The Road to Botany Bay*, p. 168.

[41] Poems from Morgan, *Shadow and Shine*.

[42] *Remembering Babylon*, pp. 110–11.

[43] For doctors' reports, see Yarra Bend Warrants ref. 2700 (1881).

[44] Boyes, 'Memoirs of Early Lardner'.

[45] See Rosen, *Madness in Society*, p. 178.

[46] Sheppard, *Lectures on Madness*, p. 13. See Rosen, *Madness in Society*, p. 190.

[47] Quoted in Sheppard, *Lectures on Madness*, p. 191.

[48] Andrews, 'The Distribution and Care of the Insane in the United States'. Quoted in Rosen, *Madness in Society*, p. 190.

[49] *Australasian Medical Gazette*, December 1883, p. 59.

[50] *Victorian Year Book*, 1884–85, p. 313.

[51] Zox Commission evidence, p. 305.

[52] See Garton, 'Bad or Mad?', p. 92.

[53] *Australasian Medical Gazette*, January 1889, p. 84.

[54] Brothers, *Early Victorian Psychiatry*, p. 14.

[55] Yarra Bend Admissions Register, ref. 7502/9, and Warrants, ref. 2700 (1881).

[56] See Garton, 'Bad or Mad?', p. 92.

[57] *Australasian Medical Gazette*, November 1883, pp. 44–5.

[58] Ibid., January 1889, p. 88.

[59] 'Patterns of psychiatric morbidity in Victoria', p. 61.

[60] *Australasian Medical Gazette*, January 1889, p. 84.

[61] Zox Commission report, Appendix to final report, p. lxxvi, quoted in Foster, 'Imperfect Victorians'.

[62] *Madness and Civilization*, pp. 261–2.

[63] Ibid., pp. x, xi. Foucault says, 'I have not tried to write the history of that language, but rather the archaeology of that silence'.

[64] Obituary, *Pastoral Review*, 15 August 1913, p. 761.

[65] *Warragul Gazette*, 7 January 1936.

[66] *A History of West Calder*, p. 49.

[67] Ibid.

[68] W. H. Oliver, 'New Zealand about 1890', quoted in Fairbairn, 'Local Community or Atomized Society?', p. 147.

[69] Fairbairn, 'Local Community or Atomized Society?', p. 149.

[70] Ibid., p. 151.

[71] Ibid., p. 153.

[72] Ibid., p. 152.

[73] Currie, 'The History of Lardner School'.

[74] Fairbairn, 'Local Community or Atomized Society?', p. 154.

[75] Veninga, 'Biography', p. 66; see also Berger, *The Sacred Canopy*.

[76] Reanney, 'Machines that Dream', p. 6.

[77] Veninga, 'Biography', p. 66.

[78] See Admissions Register, Yarra Bend Admissions Register, ref. 7417/10, and Warrants, ref. 7562/15 (1895).

[79] See Butler, *Buln Buln*, pp. 223–9.

[80] *Victorian Naturalist*, vol. 61, May 1939, pp. 14–15.

[81] Smolin, *The Life of the Cosmos*, p. 298.

[82] Reaney, 'Machines that Dream', p. 6.

[83] Jamie Grant, 'Gippsland Revisited', in Graeme Kinross-Smith and Jamie Grant, *Turn Left at Any Time with Care*.

[84] On brickmakers and brickmaking, see Malster, 'Suffolk Brickmaking', pp. 173–86; Smedley, *East Anglian Crafts*, ch. 9; Samuel, *Village Life and Village Labour*.

[85] *Ipswich Journal*, 31 July 1852.

[86] Ibid., 9 October 1852.

[87] Ibid., 12 February 1853.

[88] *Argus*, 28 December 1854. The claim may be exaggerated; see Blainey, *The Tyranny of Distance*, p. 349.

[89] Stewart, *The Early History of Bacchus Marsh Schools*, pp. 14–15, 11, 42.

Bibliography

Manuscripts and Official Sources

Boyes, Frank. 'Memoirs of Early Lardner'. La Trobe Australian Manuscript Collection, MS 9476, State Library of Victoria.

Currie, Ann Catherine. Farm diary 1873–1916 (copy). La Trobe Australian Manuscript Collection, MS10886, State Library of Victoria. The original diary is held by John Currie, grandson of Catherine and John.

Land Department Files. John Currie 299/19.20. James Currie 300/19.20. Public Records Office.

Oliver, W. H. 'New Zealand about 1890'. Unpublished Macmillan Brown Lectures, 1972.

Victorian Year Book, 1884–85. Government printer, Melbourne.

Yarra Bend Admissions Register, ref. 7502/9 and Warrants, ref. 2700 (1881); Admissions Register, ref. 7417/10 and Warrants, ref. 7562/15 (1895). Charles Brothers Museum Parkville (and now at the Victorian Public Records Office).

Zox Commission evidence, *Victorian Parliamentary Papers 1886*, 2, 7 May 1885, p. 305.

Books and Articles

Andrews, J. B. 'The Distribution and Care of the Insane in the United States', *Transactions of the International Medical Congress*, Ninth session, 1887, p. 226.

Attenborough, David, *The Private Life of Plants: a natural history of plant behaviour.* Compass Press, Boston, 1996.

Berger, Peter L. *The Sacred Canopy: elements of a sociological theory of religion.* Doubleday, New York, 1967.

Blainey, Geoffrey. *The Tyranny of Distance: how distance shaped Australia's history.* Sun Books (rev. edn), Melbourne, 1983.

Brothers, C. R. D., *Early Victorian Psychiatry 1835–1905: an account of the care of the mentally ill in Victoria.* Government printer, Melbourne, [1962 ?].

A. Bullock and O. Stallybrass (eds). *The Fontana Dictionary of Modern Thought.* Fontana, London, 1977.

Butler, Graeme. *Buln Buln: a history of the Buln Buln Shire.* Shire of Buln Buln, Drouin, 1979.

Canetti, Elias. 'Dialogue with a Cruel Partner', in *The Conscience of Words*, Seabury Press, New York, 1979.

Carter, Paul. *The Road to Botany Bay: an essay in spatial history.* Faber and Faber, London, 1987.

Copeland, Hugh. *The Path of Progress.* Shire of Warragul, 1934.

Coverdale, T. J. 'The Scrub', in *The Land of the Lyrebird.* Korumburra Shire for South Gippsland Development League, 1972 [1920].

Currie, T. B. 'The History of Lardner School'. *The Valley*, magazine of the Warragul Inspectorate, vol. 1, no. 2, 1922.

Cuthill, W. J. 'The Gippsland Road 1836–1848', *Victorian Historical Magazine*, vol. 29, February 1959, pp. 8–33.

Davison, Graeme, McCarty, J. W. and McLeary, Ailsa (eds). *Australians 1888.* Fairfax, Syme and Weldon, Sydney, 1987.

Dawkins, Richard. *River out of Eden: a Darwinian view of life.* Weidenfeld and Nicolson, London, 1995.

Dingle, Tony. *Settling.* Fairfax, Syme and Weldon, Sydney, 1984.

Duggan, Laurie. *The Ash Range.* Pan Picador, Sydney, 1987.

Eliade, Mircea. *Australian Religions.* Cornell University Press, Ithaca NY, 1973.

Fairbairn, Miles. 'Local Community or Atomized Society?', *New Zealand Journal of History*, vol. 16, October 1982, pp. 146–65.

—— 'The Rural Myth and the New Urban Frontier: an approach to New Zealand social history, 1870–1940', *New Zealand Journal of History*, vol. 9, April 1975, pp. 3–21.

Foster, Stephen. 'Imperfect Victorians: insanity in Victoria in 1888', in *Australia 1888 Bulletin* no. 8, (Monash University) pp. 97–116.

Foucault, Michel. *Madness and Civilization: a history of insanity in the Age of Reason*, trans. Richard Howard. Vintage Books, New York, 1973.

—— *The Order of Things: an archaeology of the human sciences.* Vintage Books, New York, 1973.

Garton, Stephen. 'Bad or Mad?', in *What Rough Beast?* Allen & Unwin, Sydney, 1982.

Kinross-Smith, G. and Grant J. *Turn Left at Any time With Care.* Poems by Graeme Kinross-Smith and Jamie Grant. University of Queensland Press, Brisbane, 1975.

Krupinski, Jerzy and Alexander, Lynn. 'Patterns of psychiatric morbidity in Victoria, Australia, in relation to changes in diagnostic criteria 1848–1978', *Social Psychiatry*, vol. 18, 1983.

The Land of the Lyrebird. Shire of Korumburra for the South Gippsland Development League, 1972 [1920].

Lansbury, Coral. *Arcady in Australia: the evocation of Australia in nineteenth-century English literature.* Melbourne University Press, Melbourne, 1970.

Learmonth, W. C. *A History of West Calder.* 1885.

McLeary, Ailsa. *Time and Place: essays on modern culture.* Monash Publications in History no. 10. Monash University, Melbourne, 1991.

Malcolm, Janet. *The Silent Woman, Sylvia Plath and Ted Hughes.* Picador, 1994.

Malouf, David. *Remembering Babylon.* Vintage, Sydney, 1994.

—— 'Space, Writing and Historical Identity: David Malouf talks to Paul Carter about *The Road to Botany Bay*', *Thesis Eleven*, no. 22, 1989, pp. 92–105.

Malster, Robert. 'Suffolk Brickmaking'. *Suffolk Review*, vol. 5, no. 5, 1983.

Mead, Philip. 'Topopoesis: Laurie Duggan's *The Ash Range*', *Scripsi*, vol. 4, 1987, pp. 23–40.

Merquior, J. G. *Foucault.* Fontana Press, London, 1985.

Monod, Jacques. *Chance and Necessity: an essay on the natural philosophy of modern biology*, trans. Austyn Wainhouse. Collins, London, 1972.

Morgan, Patrick. *Shadow and Shine: an anthology of Gippsland literature.* Centre for Gippsland Studies, Gippsland, 1988.

Mulvaney, D. J. and White, Peter (eds). *Australians to 1788.* Fairfax, Syme and Weldon, Sydney, 1987.

Powell, J. M. *The Public Lands of Australia Felix: settlement and land appraisal in Victoria, 1834–91.* Oxford University Press, Melbourne, 1970.

Reanney, Darryl. 'Machines that Dream'. *Age Monthly Review*, October 1983.

Rosen, George. *Madness in Society.* Routledge and Kegan Paul, London, 1968.

Samuel, Raphael (ed.). *Village Life and Labour.* Routledge and Kegan Paul, London, 1975.

Sheppard, E. *Lectures on Madness in its Medical, Legal and Social Aspects*. Churchill, London, 1973.

Smedley, Norman. *East Anglian Crafts*. Batsford, London, 1977.

Smolin, Lee. *The Life of the Cosmos*. Weidenfeld and Nicolson, London, 1997.

Stewart, Walter. *The Early History of Bacchus Marsh Schools*. Bacchus Marsh Historical Society, Bacchus Marsh, 1983.

Veninga, James F. 'Biography: self and sacred canopy', in *The Biographer's Gift, Life Histories and Humanism*. Texas A & M University Press, 1983.

Watson, Don. 'Introduction' in Laurie Duggan, *The Ash Range*. Pan Picador, Sydney, 1987.

Weller, Richard. 'The Satellites Garden', *Transition*, no. 42, 1993, pp. 45–63.

Wilde, Sally. *Forests Old, Pastures New: a history of Warragul*. Shire of Warragul, 1988.

Williams, M. 'More and Smaller is Better: Australian Rural Settlement 1788–1914', in J. M. Powell and M. Williams (eds), *Australian Space Australian Time*. Oxford University Press, Melbourne, 1975.

Index

Index